P9-DCI-248

D. Gilly

The Power
of Their Ideas

Deborah Meier

The Power of Their Ideas

Lessons for America from a Small School in Harlem

BEACON PRESS
Boston

Beacon Press
25 Beacon Street
Boston, Massachusetts 02108-2892

Beacon Press books
are published under the auspices of
the Unitarian Universalist Association of Congregations.

© 1995 by Deborah Meier
All rights reserved
Printed in the United States of America

99 98 97 96 95   8 7 6 5 4 3

Text design by Douglass G. A. Scott
Composition by Wilsted & Taylor

Library of Congress Cataloging-in-Publication Data

Meier, Deborah.
    The power of their ideas : lessons for America from a small school in
Harlem / Deborah Meier.
        p.   cm.
    ISBN 0-8070-3110-0
    1. Public schools—United States.   2. Education—United States—Aims
and objectives.   3. School management and organization—United States.
4. Teaching.   5. Educational innovations—United States.   I. Title.
LA217.2.M45   1995
372.1'0421'0973—dc20   94-40196
                                                                CIP

To my youngest collaborators,

Sarah,
Ezra,
Daniel,
and
Lilli

Contents

Preface

After thirty years of almost daily immersion in my own particular school's life, I now wake up each morning worrying about "other people's" schools, not my own. It's a big shift. It's also a good moment for looking back as well as looking forward.

Having started teaching accidentally, to pass the time until my children were old enough for me to get on with "more serious" work, I never had a grand plan. I wrote a lot about what I was seeing and learning, because it both bothered and fascinated me and writing helped me cope with it. And also, as those who know me well would tell you, because I wanted to persuade. I was being "political"—a democrat, socialist, advocate—but "in my way." My way turned out rather differently than I expected, closer to the life of the classroom and farther from the politics of education as it is usually thought of. In the end my work changed how I saw politics in its larger sense as well.

I wrote for the publications I knew best. Mostly I wrote for *Dissent* magazine, whose editor, the late Irving Howe, I so much admired. (I always waited amid much nervousness to hear his response to a manuscript, and his voice is much missed as this book goes to press.) In later years I wrote for other publications as well, particularly *The Nation*, whose remarkable editor, Victor Navasky, encouraged me to write many of the articles that subsequently formed the basis of this book. But mostly I began to speak to a wider range of audiences, trying out new ideas that sometimes made their way into print. Through it all I wrote for the parents of the children I taught and for my colleagues and the school community as a whole. I wrote memos, letters, journals, and for twenty years a weekly column for our school newsletter. My first intention was to use the offer of a contract to write a book as an opportunity to collect in one place some of these writings (with a little editing here and there) as a way to summarize before I left the immediacy of the schoolhouse.

But as I worked on it, with the prodding and patience of Wendy Strothman and Andrew Hrycyna at Beacon Press, the book became less and less a collection. Andy argued, persuaded, questioned, and advised, and was the model of a good teacher and coach. It was my West Coast colleague Mike Rose's tough critique that finally pushed it over the edge, however, and forced me to acknowledge that I had a larger argument that I wanted to make.

The idea of democracy is once again (is it ever otherwise?) in perilous danger, and as a lifelong partisan I'm out there always preaching on its behalf. So it seemed appropriate to cut and paste and revise and add in order to make the implicit explicit: democracy demands we acknowledge everyone's inalienable capacity to be an inventor, dreamer, and theorist—to count in the larger scheme of things. In the short history of modern democracy this is a belief that remains only paper thin.

Lee Shulman of Stanford once described a liberal education as a combination of "on the one hand, reverence and respect, and on the other, skepticism and doubt." Add a lot of empathy for those quite different than ourselves and it adds up to the habits of a democratic people. Not easy habits to acquire. Thus I begin, in Chapter 1, with a larger, "drier"—but crucial—discussion about the relationship between public education and democracy, and use my last twenty years in East Harlem as the primary example in the following two chapters. Both impediments and possibilities are the focus of the remainder of the book, resting always on stories and examples from my own life and the lives of those I work with.

I've had a very blessed life, both personally and professionally. While my parents—Pearl and Joe Willen—were at first chagrined at my choice of occupation, they came to be my fans and supporters, as did my husband, Fred, and my three children. Two of my children—Becky and Nicholas—now teach in elementary schools, and I continue to learn from them, as I did from their stories (and heartaches) when they were growing up. My nonteaching son, Roger, is probably the one "natural" teacher amongst us. If, as I've discovered, teaching is mostly listening and learning is mostly telling, it's not surprising. Becky, Nicky, and I are part preachers, which may partly explain our choice of teaching but has also required us to be self-consciously thoughtful about it. And then there's my brother, Paul Willen, an architect whose insistence on getting things straight makes me reread everything I write with his penetrating honesty and his very different and joyous way of seeing the world always in my mind.

I've also been lucky in colleagues and bosses. Given my stance toward administrators the latter part of that statement may surprise a lot of people. But in fact I've never worked for a principal I didn't respect, and with few exceptions the same can be said of my other immediate "bosses." For example, Ann Spero at P.S. 144M provided wise advice and an extraordinary opportunity for a novice teacher to create a mini-school of her own desires when I came back to New York City in 1967. On occasion I've had quarrels with my bosses, including a few of the many chancellors and superintendents who have come and gone over the years. Sometimes even noisy ones. But this didn't stop us; we survived them to build stronger schools and stronger relationships. Such luck doesn't come often.

And at each stage of my life important mentors and allies appeared: socialist leader and writer Mike Harrington until his untimely death, the late Lillian Weber of City College, Vito Perrone of the North Dakota Study Group and now of Harvard, Ted Sizer of Brown University and the Coalition of Essential Schools, and two of my oldest and wisest allies, Carl Shier and Ruth Jordan. There were, in addition, a host of special friends and allies—personal and collegial—who played critical roles along the way; for example, Florence Miller, who put a lot of unpaid labor into editing my writings over the years.

But it is my colleagues within the schools who have been the driving force keeping me at the typewriter for the past thirty years. Even when I've disagreed with them, I've admired them for having what it takes to do their job day in and day out. I see myself always as a teacher and so I bristle when teachers are criticized even when I believe a criticism is just. The union that represents the teachers, the UFT in New York, has always seemed my union and my quarrels with it insiders' quarrels. And above all, of course, the teachers and staff of the Central Park East schools—and the parents and students—are at the top of the list of those who have informed my work and my ideas. As I read what I've written I wince to think any one of them might disapprove or think I've missed the heart of it. This book is, after all, an attempt to tell the story of their school. I think in particular about that small band of intrepid adventurers who started the first CPE school in the late spring of 1974: Howie Budin, Digna Galarza, Lucy Matos, Liz Rodriguez, Michael Trazoff, Vivian Wallace, and Inez Wilson. Almost all are still involved in public education; three are even still at CPE. They are not responsible for my account of its history, but they are responsible for laying the foundations.

There are a few people who fit in nowhere, one-of-a-kinds—like my good friends David Rudenstine and Zina Steinberg, who played key roles in my professional career, including some roles that can never be sufficiently acknowledged, and my special neighbor Merle Gross Ginsburg. There is my appreciation for the unique support not only for our schools but for all the schools in New York City given by the founder and staff of the Aaron Diamond Foundation over so many years. Finally, I've had an extraordinary codirector, Paul Schwarz, who this year takes on the task of reshaping CPESS with his new codirector David Smith—without me! Whenever I see the two of them conferring I feel a pinch of envy, a little left out. That's as it should be since—as I hope the book suggests—being inside the life of a school means having a wonderful place from which to watch and listen to the world.

The Power
of Their Ideas

April 24

My advisees [age 13–14] on their way to a 4-day sojourn in the country: "Some people will refer to you as 'inner-city' kids," I comment. "Do you know what that means?" We live in the city, naturally, they respond. It's time to complicate. "Well, not exactly," I say, "because they wouldn't refer to the students from Dalton, which is after all ten blocks further 'in the city,' as 'inner-city.'" They got it. They followed this with a whole set of examples of euphemisms for talking about the things we're nervous about. Their sharing of ideas on this charged topic gave them a command and a power that made me feel less worried about the events we were bound to encounter over the next few days. If we could name it, we could have power over it, not it over us.

JOURNAL

October 23

I was so certain that the distinction between living and nonliving was a "simple" idea. I chose the most obvious: a rock and our gerbil. I figured I'd leave the gray areas for later. But five-year-old Darnell insists on making it difficult. Is he putting us on? "Rocks change too, and rocks move." He reminds me that on our trip to Central Park I described how the rocks had come down with the glaciers, and how they change shape over time. He won over some of the kids. They reproduce, said one: little rocks break off from big ones. I feel I'm losing the argument. So much for my neat chart.

How can we show kids that it is precisely in such ideas that important discoveries are made, rather than closing the conversation off with an "explanation." We dismiss the mistakes as cute, the accidents of ignorance; but they are at the heart of the intellectually curious mind.

JOURNAL

May 7

The struggle to lessen the gap in the realm of ideas is far more essential than early mastery of the multiplication tables (although the latter won't do any harm either); essential not only for the economic health of the nation, but imperative for its civic future. We are not predisposed to believe the startling proposition that we are all created equal.

JOURNAL

1 In Defense of Public Education

"Ooh, Daniel," a child's voice calls out, "I've got an idea." Voices pile on top of each other as one after another the children enthusiastically create imaginary worlds, share theories, and act out possibilities. As I eavesdrop on this group of four- and five-year-olds at the corner playground, their self-confident voices are a reminder of what children are like—at least sometimes, under some circumstances. It's critical to keep these voices, in all their variants, always in our heads as we think about what *could* be for all children under all circumstances.

When I started teaching four- and five-year-olds on Chicago's South Side, both the children and I were struck dumb by a world whose rules and norms we didn't understand. Why were the self-confident voices I knew so well at home and on the playground muted in the schools I taught in, I wondered? I knew that human beings are by nature generators of ideas, what I didn't understand was how it was that some children recognized the power of their ideas while others became alienated from their own genius. How did schools, in small and unconscious ways, silence these persistent playground intellectuals? Could schools, if organized differently, keep this nascent power alive, extend it, and thus make a difference in what we grow up to be? The constraints that poverty and racism impose on the lives of children might be real, but could schools loosen rather than tighten them? These questions—and their implications—have kept me close to the classroom for thirty years, including twenty as the teacher-director of a public elementary and high school in New York City's East Harlem.

My own experiences over the past three decades have reinforced my optimism regarding the possibilities of making dramatic changes in the ways schools operate, changes that can transform the lives of children. All kids are indeed capable of generating powerful ideas; they can rise to the occasion. It turns out that ideas are not luxuries gained at the expense of the 3 R's, but instead enhance them. And it turns out that public schools, in new and different forms, are the best vehicle for nourishing the extraordinary untapped capacities of all our children. The question is not, Is it possible to educate all children well? but rather, Do we want to do it badly enough?

But there's a radical—and wonderful—new idea here—the idea that every citizen is capable of the kind of intellectual competence previously attained by only a small minority. It was only after I had begun to teach that public rhetoric gave even lip service to the notion that all children could and should be inventors of their own theories, critics of other people's ideas, analyzers of evidence, and makers of their own personal marks on this most complex world. It's an idea with revolutionary implications. If we take it seriously.

This book is about taking this vision of education and human possibility seriously. The task of creating environments where all kids can experience the power of their ideas requires unsettling not only our accepted organization of schooling and our unspoken and unacknowledged agreement about the purposes of schools. Taking this task seriously also means calling into question our definitions of intelligence and the ways in which we judge each other. And taking it seriously means accepting public responsibility for the shared future of the next generation. It's a task for all of us, not just school people or policymakers or even parents alone. The stakes are enormous, and the answers within our reach.

Because we are talking about all children, an education that is public is the necessary, albeit not sufficient, precondition for making it happen. If a significant number of Americans abandon public education—either out of lethargy or by opting for private religious, ethnic, or elite academies—we risk turning public schools into schools of last resort. Even those committed to public schooling can be driven out by a slow and steady erosion of public support and the increasing attractions of subsidized private solutions—vouchers, private charters, etc. To stay with public school begins to sound sentimental, the sacrifice of one's own children for the sake of public policy—at least for those with a chance to get out. The net effect undermines the public's will to create a first-class system of public education. We risk turning the current popular mantra "all children can learn" into a cynical two-tiered vision of what's good enough for "ours" versus what's good enough for "theirs."

But there's something else that's driving my commitment to public education—my passion for democracy and my fears for its future. Intolerance and dogmatism, narrow and often murderous national and religious loyalties, and the casual acceptance of the most grotesque inequities have made democracy's promise seem at times improbable rather than inevitable. Oddly enough, having defeated two major threats to democracy—fascism and communism—we seem less not more sure about democracy's virtues.

When I sent my own three children off to school for the first time, more than thirty years ago, I took public education for granted. Like most Americans, I thought of democracy as a stage in the natural progression from lower to higher forms of being and assumed the world was poised on the eve of a fulsome embrace of democratic norms. It would not be an uninterrupted string of victories but the direction was clear—if we didn't blow ourselves up. Public education seemed a necessary and secure part of this American dream of steady progress. One of the features that sold us on our particular row house on Chicago's multiracial, largely low-income South Side was that it was across the street from a local school. While a few of our neighbors who were on the faculty of the

University of Chicago sent their children to its private Lab School, the rest of us had no doubts about the neighborhood public school. It just was the thing to do.

When my parents moved into New York City in the late 1930s they sent my brother and me to a private progressive school. Much as I generally respected my parents' values and their approach to child rearing, by the time I had my own children I unhesitantly disagreed. I recalled how once a year we all attended a ceremony to celebrate the founding of our private school. Each year we were told the stirring story of the founder's wish to create a school for working men and women, to teach the arts of democracy in the interest of an egalitarian vision of society. That not a single working man's child now attended our school was acknowledged, oddly enough, as a sign of the school's success. I wanted my children to be educated in schools that saw their mission as tackling that founder's original dream. But, principles aside, I also saw my parents' choice of a private school as foolish and unnecessary.

Today I am more sympathetic to my parents' decision than I was when I began parenthood. In retrospect, I made the decision to send our kids to public school a bit cavalierly, without much knowledge or thought about the details of public school life (I had not yet begun to teach), and thus without much reflection on the ways in which I had truly been advantaged by my schooling. Schools can squelch intelligence, they can foster intolerance and disrespect, they affect the way we see ourselves in the pecking order. But that's precisely why we cannot abandon our public responsibility to all children, why we need a greater not a lesser commitment to public education. Children grow up, and the kinds of habits of mind they bring to both the workplace and the polling place will determine our common fate. It's quite possible that American society can develop a viable economy that ignores the fate of vast numbers of its citizens, one not dependent upon a universally well-educated public. But only at a cost to democracy itself.

* * *

Schools dependent upon private clienteles—schools that can get rid of unwanted kids or troublemaker families, exclude on the basis of this or that set of beliefs, and toss aside the "losers"—not only can avoid the democratic arts of compromise and tolerance but also implicitly foster lessons about the power of money and privilege, a lesson already only too well known by every adolescent in America. In schools that are public, citizens are joined by right, not by privilege. The critics of public institutions, of course, often decry all this talk about rights—from the rights of the handicapped to the rights of teenagers to wear outrageous clothes. Rights get messy and litigious. Democracy is not always convenient, and rights do require sorting out. Neither equity, civil rights, nor mutual respect for the ideas of others are always the winners even in public institutions—far from it—but public schooling shifts the odds in favor of such democratic principles.

In schools kids sit down next to their classmates, whoever they are. Parents proudly come together at school concerts, weep together at graduations, and congregate in times of crisis at public hearings and PTA meetings. Public schools therefore offer opportunities for a sense of community otherwise sorely missing, for putting faces and names to people we might otherwise see as mere statistics or categories. They teach us how one conducts oneself in public—for better or worse. Reading through small-town newspapers reminds us that democratic "conversation" is often loud and rude, and sometimes leaves scars and neighborly hostility. But if democracy survives such hostility it's because we assume we're members of a common club, stuck with each other.

Public schools can train us for such political conversation across divisions of race, class, religion, and ideology. It is often in the clash of irreconcilable ideas that we can learn how to test or revise ideas, or invent new ones. Both teachers and students need to search for metaphors that work across ideological, historical, and personal differences. We cannot assume everyone will react the same way to the theory of evolution, the "discovery" of America, the Gulf War, or the value of "life-style" choices. Differences make things complicated.

But dealing with the complicated is what training for good citizenship is all about. Ideas—the ways we organize knowledge—are the medium of exchange in democratic life, just as money is in the marketplace.

We just cannot afford to give up. Democracy is based on our power to influence by our public statements and actions what we want the future to look like. It depends on people's ability to believe that money alone doesn't do *all* the talking. Our current state of anger at public schools is in many ways an anger over our loss of control over important decisions affecting our communities. But if we abandon public schooling we have lost one more vehicle for controlling our future. Privatizing removes schools from democratic control. Why bother, after all, to debate what direction we want the future to take if we no longer have a voice in what are arguably the most important institutions for shaping that future—our schools? The old-fashioned principle of "one for all and all for one" will be hard to regain once abandoned.

There are wounded children and families amidst us who can barely imagine that talk about "all for one" is anything but a trick to catch them off guard. I battle such cynicism among students and their families. Disbelief in human solidarity appears among white and black children, rich and poor. For many children and their families schools are one of the few institutions that can provide the experience of membership in an enlarged common community, and it's the absence of community that seems for some a matter of life and death. It's precisely in search of such community, for example, that some African-American families have opted out of public schools in favor of all-black private schools.

Giving up on public schooling as our accepted norm would mean leaving our nation's children in the hands of unknown baby-sitters with unknown agendas. To want to know who the baby-sitter is and what he or she is up to is not a right versus left issue. And this is true not only with respect to one's own child, but also with respect to our collective children. We have a legitimate role in setting the agenda for our own individual children; we have an equally important role in setting the agenda for our children at large. It matters a lot whether the schools in which our youth spend eighteen years foster democratic or undemocratic values, for example. That's not a private matter, each to his or her "own thing." A school system in which students must come together with others who are different may or may not further any one individual family's life goals, but it holds the potential to further our common goals as a democratic society. If we want to chart the future together these "details" of what goes on in our schools matter. It won't always be easy to get the balance between the private rights of families and the public rights of the larger community quite right; but turning it all over to either one or the other appears easier only in the short run.

This is not the first crisis for public education. A 1918 U.S. government–commissioned report on public education spoke familiarly to the erosion of family life, disappearing fathers, working mothers, the decline of religious institutions, changes in the workplace, and millions of newly arrived immigrants as sources of the crisis facing public life and public education. The educators and public officials of the day created a system that would absorb these millions into the vastly expanding factories of America. They had an answer; they created the modern public school system, with its two tracks—one ending long before high school graduation with minimal academic goals and the other aimed at a small college-bound elite. For seventy years we've fiddled, papering over this duality as best we could with the comprehensive high school, and rarely serving either of its two tiers well. But we haven't given up, nor abandoned our public responsibility for the education of the young.

The idea of education as a shared public responsibility is more critical now than it was in 1918, and more critical than in my own youth a half-century ago. The formal and informal institutions that were once accessible to the majority of children and that grounded the young in a society of responsible adults are missing for most, at precisely the moment they are most needed. Face-to-face meeting places such as political clubs, union halls, and settlement houses have all but disappeared. These were not only places of nurturance, but places where we learned skills, felt safe enough to take needed risks, learned to believe in the future. Only schools remain.

In addition, the role of the school has vastly expanded. Young people are now required to attend school for twelve long years or more, rather than the mere five or six that was customary in 1918. Students do not have the option of moving into the "real world" at the age of fourteen as the vast majority once did (or of respectably skipping school at harvest time). Quite aside from their intellectual potency or their certification role, schools thus mark youngsters ever more deeply with their implicit values—not always those they intended to convey. Youngsters learn their place in the social order and develop a system of responses to their placement that are hard to dislodge. They form "an attitude" toward work, adults, the larger public setting, and what counts and what doesn't on the basis of schools. Schools still matter even more than TV in telling us who we are and can be.

Under these circumstances, the question of what kids are to be exposed to and how they and their families are to be treated in school takes on new dimensions. It's time to invent a twenty-first century answer, rather than just nibbling away at the old 1918 one. We need as many opportunities as possible for hearing and persuading each other that what's good for one might be good for all, that my child's interests are not a threat to yours. And we need to do this not just once, but over and over again. It's that important. Only out of such debate will we build new and better kinds of schools.

It will be difficult. We're just now learning how to create schools that work for everyone, just beginning to work out ways to do it on the scale needed. Until recently we were hardly surprised (nor were we concerned) that the socioeconomic and educational history of a family was overwhelmingly the best predictor of school success— more statistically reliable than any test devised. At the school in East Harlem where I've worked for the past twenty-one years, we've shown that it is possible to break that pattern—and not for just a few "exceptional" children. We're far from alone. What we've discovered is that accepting the challenge to break with the past assumes a respect for our fellow beings and their capacities that does not come easily or naturally to most of us. We need not only to accept some new ideas, but to dislodge many of our old ones. It's not surprising that so many families, so many teachers, and so many politicians are looking for an escape, urging us to retreat to an imagined past where everyone succeeded—with their McDuffey readers, teacher-proof daily lesson plans, and desks that faced forward all in a row—or to opt out altogether into their separate ethnic or religious enclaves. We're not accustomed to recognizing the power of each other's ideas; it's easier to take flight.

If we abandon a system of common schools—through apathy or privatization—we deprive everyone, not just the least advantaged, of the kind of clash of ideas that will make us all more powerful. We're a nation that loves a good fight; fighting with ideas rather than fists or guns or nasty sound bites could be a welcome relief. More importantly, reinventing our public schools could provide an exciting opportunity to use our often forgotten power to create imaginary worlds, share theories, and act out possibilities. This time not just on the playground but in all the varied public arenas in which we meet with our fellow citizens.

Schools embody the dreams we have for our children. All of them. These dreams must remain public property.

February 16

My secretary interrupted our meeting three times today. A man from the Board insisted on knowing our "bell schedule." I told her to tell him (a) we had no bells and (b) there were three schools in the building and each had different schedules. He wouldn't be put off. So I told her to tell him they went off "every hour on the hour." He was satisfied. A report is now on file somewhere containing this data. Why? And why don't I remember to give the phony answers they want immediately? Probably if we tracked the history of each of these mindless requests we'd find it originated as a response to some ancient "scandal." In a system this large there's always one.

JOURNAL

January 29

Once again someone wants hard data on our success. As a purist about data I can't compress it into the needed two sentences. Compared to New York City data re attendance, graduation rates, test scores, college acceptances, it's so staggeringly high that I suppose precision isn't necessary.

Judy came in with her infant. She's one of four CPESSers who've had babies. How we agonize! We get anxious when the girls act so thrilled with a classmate's baby. On the other hand, motherhood is wonderful. If a youngster has chosen that route, however thoughtlessly, do we want to be her enemy? Is it contagious? Is that what I fear? So I hug her, too. And feel joy.

JOURNAL

December 3

Came back from Carmela's funeral. The school's steady attention to Carmela and her family as she lay dying for nearly a year can't happen in a school five times our size. Yet death surrounds our kids. If death doesn't count, does life?

Friends in other schools claim they see the despair; or is it the symptoms they see: violence, death, pregnancy, drugs. We see less of these—because we're smaller? more supportive?—and when we do, we think we can act, "do" something. Does that make our kids seem more "normal"—joyous, giggly, flirtatious, friendly? Have we created enough of an internal culture to sustain hopefulness at least between 9:00 and 3:00? Is it mostly being small and intimate enough to pay attention? It's not that we've figured out how to make all our subjects interesting or relevant or our assessment authentic. Although we try. But the place itself is interesting and authentic. I used to say that I learned most of what I knew as a kid in the company of people who were talking "over my head." I think that's how human beings naturally learn. Maybe the kids learn more here accidentally than on purpose. There are so many conversations going on.

JOURNAL

2 Central Park East: An Alternative Story

In the spring of 1991, Central Park East, located in New York's East Harlem, graduated its first high school students. Most of the graduates had spent at least six years with us, while some had been with us since they were four or five years old. Their achievement was heralded not only by the families of the graduates and their teachers, but by others from throughout the country who came to celebrate with us. Our school, once a lonely maverick, was now one among many schools in New York City able to demonstrate how all children could meet high standards of intellectual achievement within a public school setting, and part of a national movement to change the face of American education.

Defending public education is difficult, but the best defense is by example. City schools seem to many to be especially hopeless, and many who would probably love to support public education feel it's romantic to hold on to dreams such as ours. The story of how the Central Park East schools came to be and how they work generates possibilities that can change the way we think about all our schools, rich and poor, rural or urban. Here are some particulars.

Central Park East is in fact four public schools working in close collaboration with each other under all the constraints of the public school system, but without all of the problems that plague many others.

The data on the Central Park East elementary and secondary schools is not in dispute. The CPE population is roughly equivalent to a cross sampling of New York City. The majority of students are African-American and Latino, most are low-income or poor, and they experience a full range of academic strengths and handicaps. Of the first seven graduating classes of CPE elementary school (1977–1984), 85 percent received regular diplomas and another 11 percent got GEDs. This compares to roughly 50 percent citywide. Furthermore, two thirds of those who graduated from high school prior to the opening of our own secondary school had gone on to college. And the statistics held across race and class lines. In 1991, the Central Park East Secondary School topped this impressive showing. While some students moved and a few transferred, fewer than 5 percent of those who started with us in ninth grade dropped out along the way. And not only did the rest graduate with regular diplomas, but 90 percent went directly on to college and stayed there. These figures for 1991 have held up for each subsequent graduating class. And the graduates of 1994 outstripped their pre-decessors in quality of work achieved and colleges attended. We've gotten better and so have they.

The Central Park East schools follow in the tradition of many of New York's independent private schools, a tradition few believed was appropriate for public education. They are places that success-fully embody a conception of education that challenges most urban public schools' low and trivial expectations. Each of the four schools offers a rich and interesting curriculum full of powerful ideas and experiences aimed at inspiring its students with the desire to know more, a curriculum that sustains students' natural drive to make sense of the world and trusts in their capacity to have an impact upon it. The CPE schools are places where "teachers with the pas-sion of the amateur and the competence of the professional" thrive, to quote David Ruenzel in an article on what African-American par-ents are seeking from private all-black schools.

Even now, twenty years later, as I see our work assuming new forms and shapes as it spreads to schools throughout the city, I nervously worry, Are we a fluke?

For most of the staff and many of our parents, well-wishers, and friends, the success of Central Park East is a dream come true. A rather fragile dream, it has been tossed about by many of the ill winds of this city's tumultuous politics. Today, however, it would take an unusually strong storm to uproot us or break us—or even to bend us very much. Our parents and alumni/ae are, of course, our first line of defense. But today we are also surrounded by powerful outside friends and by dozens of sister schools struggling collaboratively to make a common dream come true not just for one small group of students in one of the city's thirty-two districts but throughout this system of a million students. We are filled with the heady vision that perhaps even in our lifetimes we can make schools like ours accessible to any student and family that wants this kind of education.

It wasn't always so. What has allowed this to happen is a combination of imaginative public policy initiated by a few brave, well-situated officials who made the experiment even possible; specific reproducible ways of organizing schools and of getting teachers, students, and families to work together; a small crew of teachers who were ready to take the risks and seize the opportunities; and a group of families either desperate enough or eager enough to give it a chance. Our singular success depended on complementary larger efforts: a districtwide effort throughout East Harlem to create a network of small elementary and junior high schools and a citywide effort to create a network of alternative high schools—public schools of choice for families and faculties. We are, in fact, just one of nearly forty options available to families in East Harlem's District 4, aside from the regular neighborhood or zoned elementary schools, and one of several dozen alternative high schools that have been nurtured by the special Alternative High School Division situated within the Central Board of Education since 1984.

Today, both District 4's example and the work of the alternative high schools are proliferating like wildfire; a whole series of subsequent developments have finally—after nearly twenty years of quiet growth and gestation—caught on. For example, during 1993 and 1994 nearly forty small schools that involve high-school-age students opened under varied auspices, including a dozen designed to replace two unsuccessful large neighborhood comprehensive high schools. All involved some form of faculty and student choice and far greater autonomy and self-governance than the system had previously allowed. Many involved new partnerships with other community groups. None has fit in easily. They are still severely handicapped by a system that is struggling to reexamine what must change, root and branch, if these success stories are to become the norm. But many people are beginning to think that maybe they too can "found" their own schools. From top to bottom the system is readying itself for change. The genie is out of the bottle and it will be hard to put it back.

The founding of the first CPE school in 1974 came at a most inauspicious time, just as New York City's school system was forced to lay off more than fifteen thousand teachers and to close virtually all elementary school libraries and most music and art programs. This bloodletting simultaneously crushed both a thriving parent movement bent on decentralization and efforts by teachers to redesign curriculum and classroom life based on a new look at the nature of teaching and learning. These blows came on top of a divisive battle that pitted a mostly white teaching force against minority communities and one set of parents against another—the 1967 and 1968 teacher strikes and parent boycotts. Progressive educators in particular suffered during the aftermath of the strike and the devastating budget cuts; conventional wisdom said that "openness" was "through" (and discredited) and many of the young teachers and new programs that had carried the progressive message, already badly divided by the strike, were subsequently hardest hit by the layoffs.

In the spring of 1974, when Anthony Alvarado, the new superintendent in East Harlem's District 4, invited me to start a small elementary school in one wing of P.S. 171, it seemed a most unlikely offer. School District 4, serving one of the city's poorest communities, was led by a politically divided and factionalized school board. Most students were Latino, but the community included a growing African-American population. It was educationally on the bottom, with test scores that placed it last out of the thirty-two city districts.

Naturally I accepted the offer. Who could refuse? After struggling for years to make my beliefs fit into a system that was organized on quite different (and hostile) principles, after spending considerable energy looking for cracks, operating on the margins, compromising at every turn, the prospect that the district bureaucracy would organize itself to support alternative ideas and practices was irresistible. Having been out of the classroom for three years, working in a City College–initiated program as an adviser to teachers who were interested in change, I was also eager to have a home again, to be back in the classroom. I was being offered a chance to focus not on bureaucratic red tape but on the intractable issues of education—the ones that really interested me and many of the teachers I knew well. The question for us was how the children at the bottom of America's social ladder could use their schools to develop rather than stunt their intellectual potential, how to provide at public expense for the least advantaged what the most advantaged bought privately for their own children.

But this was not a time in history—the mid-1970s—for having large visions. We would be satisfied if we could create an interesting place where important questions could be asked and explored. I met with Alvarado, collected a core group of experienced colleagues, and gradually began to believe that he meant what he said: that we could build a school just the way we wanted. The total allocation of funds (per-pupil costs) would have to be comparable to what was spent on any other school, and our staff would have to meet the usual requirements of the city, the state, and the union contract. (Years later, a diligent researcher proved we had actually received slightly less in public resources than other schools.) We would be exempt from no city or state regulations. Beyond that, however, the district would support us in doing things our way.

We were all a little wary. The staff included veterans of experimental programs which had been destroyed by budgetary cuts and unsympathetic administrations, teachers who'd been caught working in schools whose philosophies they strongly opposed, former teachers who had left demoralized and exhausted but were willing to try again, supervisors who wanted to go back into the classroom, and a few colleagues fresh from student teaching. Most had experienced the fatigue that comes from cutting corners on the things that truly matter in order to meet the endlessly proliferating mandated programs and mandated accountability schemes.

We began small and carefully. We put all our resources into our classrooms. As teacher-director I had a regular full-time class of second- and third-graders. (We bought an answering machine to deal with the office.) We wanted no "we" versus "they" in our community. Creating a democratic community was both an operational and an inspirational goal. While we were in part the products of what was called "open education," our roots went back to early progressive traditions, with their focus on the building of a democratic community, on education for full citizenship and egalitarian ideals. We looked upon both John Dewey and Jean Piaget as our mentors. We were intrigued by the way individuals structured their thinking, as well as by the role of the community, the social setting, in the learning process. For us, a democratic community was the nonnegotiable purpose of good schooling.

Most of the original staff, six teachers and one paraprofessional (three of the teachers were white, two black, and one Latino), were students of Lillian Weber's at the City College Workshop Center. We came out of a tradition that was increasingly uneasy about the individualistic focus of much of what was being called "open" or "progressive." To us progressive education was not only child-centered but community-centered as well. We adopted Lillian's use of the word "personalized," and learned from her thoughtful reminders that diversity among people strengthens the larger community. We saw subject matter in broad terms, as the powerful "stuff" that makes up our common world. Lillian rooted the new for us within the old; she warned us to look for the strengths within traditions we might otherwise reject out of hand. She taught us about looking for cracks in the system, always being advocates for the children, and above all she demanded intellectual toughness of teachers, not just of kids.

We were unhappy about the focus on breaking everything down into discrete skills rather than introducing strong subject matter, a focus that we saw in many of the "innovative" schools that labeled themselves open or progressive. One longed for a simple fact or a little memorization of poetry in some of these "modern" classrooms! My children's best and favorite teacher, I noticed, thought of herself as a traditionalist in response to many of the terms then current in educational debate. "Personalization" had been interpreted by too many to mean only that children could acquire skills at their own pace, and "individualism" and "active learning" as ways of placating restless or angry kids. (No wonder many African-American teachers and parents thought progressivism a cop-out, a way of avoiding, not confronting, the challenge. While many people have resisted progressive educational theories for many reasons, noted African-American educator Lisa Delpit points out that there has been something particularly frustrating to nonwhite teachers and parents in the seeming avoidance of "direct" instruction, as though if we waited long enough children would discover everything on their own; what they felt was that this represented either a patronizing attitude or a lack of sufficient care.)

In contrast, we saw children being driven into dumbness by a failure to challenge their curiosity, to build on their natural drive toward competence. We thought adults had important things to teach children, not just a mission to get out of their way. Our kind of classroom was not stocked with ditto fill-in sheets but literally full of stuff: books of every sort, paints as well as paintings, plants, animals, broken radios to repair—things. The curriculum we sought was both conceptual and *tangible*. We wanted children to fall in love as we had with stories of the past, including their own; we wanted schools that would evoke a sense of wonder. Building such schools, we thought, required strong and interesting adults who could exercise their own curiosity and judgment, who knew, as learning theorist Eleanor Duckworth put it, what "the having of wonderful ideas" was all about.

We also saw schools as examples of the possibilities of democratic community, and what we meant by this was continuously under debate and review. It wasn't simply a question of governance structures, and certainly not a matter of extending the vote to four-year-olds. Although classroom life could certainly include more participation by children in decisions than traditional schools allowed, we saw it as even more critical that the school life of adults be democratic. It seemed unlikely that we could foster values of community in our classrooms unless the adults in the school had significant rights over their own workplace. For us, democracy implied that people should have a voice not only in their own individual work, but in the work of others as well. Finally, we saw collaboration and mutual respect among staff, parents, students, and the larger community as a part of what we meant by calling our experiment democratic.

We knew that we were tackling many difficult issues at once. Time for planning and reflection was insufficient. We had a lean staff and no sister schools in 1974. But we saw no way to put any of these issues off until "later." Looking back, we were so euphoric that we had the energy of twice our number. Besides, we thought we knew exactly what we were after.

We started our school with fewer than a hundred students—kindergarten, first and second grades, and a few third-graders. At the superintendent's request, we recruited outside the usual channels, in part so that we wouldn't threaten other schools in the district and in part because one of Alvarado's goals was to increase the district's pupil population, thus guarding against being required to close more school buildings.

We had no academic entrance qualifications; we took all who said that this was what they wanted. We insisted that parents (or grandparents, aunts, older siblings) visit before signing up, and we considered it our job to enlist their collaboration. Families came to us then, as they do today, for many reasons. Many families came because they had been told by Head Start teachers, social workers, or principals that their children needed something different, that they were too fidgety, noisy, withdrawn, or hard to manage. In short, many families came to us because experts claimed that their children would have trouble in a traditional school. Some came because their children were already having trouble in other schools or because older siblings had had trouble in the past. (We reminded uneasy parents that they had a right to stay in their neighborhood schools if they preferred, in order to avoid becoming known as the place other schools could "dump" their failures or troublemakers.)

Some families came because they heard us speak and just liked the way we sounded—caring (they told us later), open, friendly, committed. Some came because they had friends who knew us professionally and some because they were looking for a different kind of school for philosophical reasons. Yet even among those who chose us because of our presumed beliefs, there was often confusion about what those beliefs were. Some thought, for example, that this would be a parent-run school; some thought we didn't believe in any restrictions on children's freedom.

One of our primary reasons for starting the school—although we didn't often admit it—was our personal desire for greater autonomy as teachers. We spoke a lot about democracy, but we were also just plain sick and tired of having to waste so much time and energy negotiating with school officials over what seemed like commonsense requests, worrying about myriad rules and regulations, being forced to compromise on so many of our beliefs. We came together with our own visions of what teaching could be if only *we* had control. We saw parents as crucial, but viewed their input as advisory. Parental choice was in part a way we imagined we'd increase our autonomy.

While eschewing formal teacher/parent co-governance, we knew that good early childhood education requires authentic forms of collaboration between the school and the family. This is a matter not only of political principle but also of educational practicality, and it motivated us from the start to work hard to build a family-oriented school. We wanted a school in which children would feel safe. Intellectual risk taking requires safety; children who are suspicious of a school's agenda cannot work up to their potential. For the school to be safe, children needed to know that their parents trusted us. It was that simple. Hard to create, perhaps, but essential.

Our experience suggested that a strong school culture requires that most decisions be struggled over and made by those directly responsible for implementing them, not by representative bodies handing down dictates for others to follow. We felt the same way whether the representative bodies were composed of kids, parents, or fellow teachers. Representative bodies are surely a legitimate form of democracy, just not very effective for the kind of school culture we were trying to create. In practice, creating a culture of this sort meant that only those few parents who were prepared to join the staff and school on a fairly regular basis got fully "represented" in the schoolwide decisions that counted, not a solution that always satisfied all parents or teachers at CPE. The CPE approach placed a heavier burden on public school choice as a form of parental empowerment, on the judicious use of advisory boards and parent councils for input, on openness and accessibility, and above all on the power and frequency of individual school/family relationships. It also called for rethinking the staffing of a school so that the gap between parents and school would be bridged in part by teachers who "think like parents," in particular like the parents whose children attend our schools. This meant always trying to recruit and maintain more staff, for example, who were African-American and Latino.

We stumbled a lot in those early years over such issues. We fought among ourselves. Personal autonomy and communal decision making didn't always go well together. We were teachers with strong personalities, used to going our own way and annoyed at having to convince others about pedagogical issues—colleagues or parents. In our former, less compatible traditional schools we had grown accustomed to closing our doors and secretly doing what we wanted. Sometimes we regretted we hadn't created a collection of one-room schoolhouses!

The struggle to preserve personal autonomy often overwhelmed the needs of the community. We discovered that staff decision making was time consuming. It often seemed it would be easier if there were someone clearly "above" to blame in order to shortcut arguments. We weren't wholly comfortable with the idea that arguing was a healthy aspect of democratic life and certainly wished that we were better at doing it! It was hard, too, to engage in arguments among ourselves without frightening parents and raising doubts about our professionalism. We were often exhausted by the things that mattered least to us.

By the end of the second year, schisms within our own ranks, aided and abetted by a group of dissident parents, required rethinking and reorganization of the school. A largely personal power struggle with one key and charismatic colleague, combined with dissatisfaction on the part of some parents who sought a more directly parent-controlled school, shook us to our roots. Only the steady support of the district, the backing of the vast majority of parents, and the existence of alternative choices for the dissatisfied cut our losses and made this brief rebellion a blip in our history. (In subsequent years other schools like ours have all, we've discovered, experienced similar moments. Crises are part of the life of such institutions and are too often covered up rather than learned from.)

The experience led me to make some crucial decisions regarding the future organization of Central Park East, decisions necessary if I were to remain even its titular leader (the title being "teacher-director"). The central change involved my becoming somewhat more of a traditional leader, with time to "lead." The staff also voted for less sharing of administrative tasks, so we got rid of our phone-answering machine and hired someone for the office. Two teachers left (one of whom subsequently returned and later became the leader of a CPE school), along with about a dozen parents out of around a hundred and fifty.

We remained a "staff-run" school, but not a principal-less collective, as we had originally envisioned. Although formally I was still "just" a teacher, I was no longer full-time in a classroom of kids. The bottom line remained: the staff (and the parents who chose to join us) continued to be central to all decisions, big and small, the final plenary body directing the life of the school. Nothing was or has ever been "undiscussable," although we have learned not to discuss everything—at least not all the time. This has actually meant more time for discussing those issues that concern us most: how children learn, how our classes really work, what changes we ought to be making and on what basis. We have also become better observers of our own practice, better collectors of information, documenters of practice as well as users of expertise. We thus have more to bring to the collective table. Yet the complexities of school governance—by whom and how decisions are made, questions of "we" and "they"— still crop up from time to time to bedevil us. How teachers can take collective responsibility for supervising each other, for determining school rules, disciplinary consequences, and school schedules, as well as for the trickier issue of standards and evaluation, while also maintaining sufficient classroom autonomy and focus has not been resolved. We console ourselves with Winston Churchill's paean to democracy as "the worst form of government except all those other forms that have been tried from time to time."

As we have grown in our understanding and in practical skills, we have also been obliged to reexamine the relationships between school and family. Today we understand better the many, often subtle ways in which schools can undermine family support systems, can undercut children's faith in their parents as educators and in their community as a worthy place. Given our good intentions this has not always been easy for us to notice. Our assumption of expertise and our concern lest parents and grandparents "misteach" children this or that school skill can widen the very gap we are so busy trying to close. We complain later when they wearily pull back, if not altogether out, but what has our role been in this withdrawal? We were determined to keep exploring new ways to make connections. Although we have not changed our beliefs about the value of "literature-based" and "whole-language" approaches to teaching reading in contrast to basal readers or formal phonics, for instance, we have become more supportive of parents whose home instruction differs from ours. In math, learning how to subtract in the old ways as well as in the new ways may even be an advantage, we now argue. Is it so terrible to fall back on such "anachronisms" as borrowing from the tens column? Kids can adapt to a variety of methods. As psycholinguist Frank Smith wisely notes, "In the two-thousand-year recorded history of reading instruction, as far as I have been able to discover, no one has devised a method of teaching reading that has not proved a success with some children."

In short, we give less advice, are less prescriptive. We try not to suggest obvious "solutions," like having a quiet homework area or buying an alarm clock. We listen with a more critical ear to what we say to parents, wondering how we would hear it as parents ourselves and about how children may interpret the relationship as well. We invite students, four-year-olds and eighteen-year-olds, to join teacher/parent conferences, viewing such conferences as joint school/family problem-solving sessions in which all parties share information. Since relationships take time to build, we keep kids and teachers together for two years when we can.

As we became more secure with our way of working, District 4 was expanding its network of choices. In the fall of 1974 we were one of only two alternatives. Within a half-dozen years there were more than fifteen "alternative concept" schools, mostly on the junior high level, where schooling had most glaringly broken down. Today fifty-two schools occupying twenty District 4 buildings, with a total population of about thirteen thousand students mostly under the age of fourteen, comprise a group of alternative schools that is bigger than the vast majority of school districts throughout the nation.

This represents a sweeping change that required ignoring the assumption that a building equals a school. Every building in the district soon housed several schools, each with its own leadership, budget, parent body, curricular focus, organization, and philosophy. Our original site held three schools—the neighborhood school, our own elementary school, and a small alternative junior high. (Most of the new junior highs were located in elementary school buildings, and former junior high buildings were gradually turned to multiple use as well.) As a result, the schools were small and their staffs and parents were associated with them largely by choice. Generally the building contained only one "official" principal, which sometimes caused quarrels and tensions. To this day, unlike the alternative high schools, none of District 4's small schools are acknowledged as "real"; only the original twenty school buildings show up on centrally controlled forms, budget allocations, or organizational charts. The schools mostly suffer from this undercover existence, although there are occasional benefits to not being noticed "downtown."

The Central Park East's schools have always had a predominantly African-American (nearly half) and Latino (about a third) student population. They are also among the few district schools that have maintained a steady white population, as large as about 25 percent in the elementary schools and closer to 10 percent in the high school. (The population of District 4 is about 60 percent Latino, 35 percent African-American, and less than 5 percent white and "other.") Well over half of our students have always qualified for free lunches, and some 20 percent meet the state requirements for being labeled "handicapped," thus qualifying for special state funds. Researchers investigating our population generally conclude our students are at least as "at risk" as New York City's general population, although more heterogeneous than the average East Harlem school.

In the beginning, these ratios came about largely by chance, but the 20 to 25 percent white population in the elementary schools has been maintained by choice—by both the local school board and CPE. As mentioned before, one of the district's motivations for starting new alternative schools was to offset its declining student population, and so "outsiders" were more than welcome. Federal funds for integration were part of the lure for the district as they encouraged us to maintain our white population. Already the belief in the possibility of school integration was losing its power and CPE's integrated enrollment met with a mixed reception in East Harlem, some resenting the white children who traveled to our schools and took seats that might otherwise have gone to Latino or African-American children. In general, the CPE schools have sought to maintain heterogeneity without having too many fixed rules or complex machinery. In the mid-1980s we adopted a lottery system that favors neighborhood students and ensures fairness; it also avoids handling large masses of visitors and applicants. The one exception to the lottery is that the CPE schools accept all siblings, to preserve our family orientation.

Central Park East grew from one school to four mostly because we were inundated with applications. Turning anyone down was painful, lottery or no. In 1980 an annex opened in P.S. 109, a few blocks south of the original. It soon assumed its own separate status. Several years later a third, River East, opened on 115th and the East River. Thus by 1984 Central Park East had become three schools, each with 250 students, each with its own style and character, yet united in basic ways. Then, in 1984 at our tenth anniversary celebration, Theodore Sizer, a former dean of the Harvard School of Education and then (as now) at Brown University, congratulated the school for its impressive history and asked, "Why not a Central Park East secondary school? Why stop at sixth grade?"

We agreed. In fact Sizer's presence at our celebration was not an accident. We had read excerpts from his just-published *Horace's Compromise*, part of a larger study of American high schools. It resonated. Here was a highly respected educational guru who spoke our language. We knew that starting a secondary school was a good idea, but until the early 1980s we had shied away from it. It seemed too dangerous, and we were early childhood experts, anyway. Some of our critics had said that a nurturing elementary school wouldn't prepare students to cope with the "real world"—wouldn't nurturing be even less legitimate in a high school? In fact, a commissioned study of our graduates had proven our critics wrong about elementary school, and our good sense suggested it would prove them wrong about a high school. Regardless of race or social class, the graduating sixth-graders of the CPE schools had handled the real world remarkably well. They had coped. The statistics amazed even us.

But our graduates had unhappy stories to tell about the high school experiences they'd had after CPE, stories not about being ed-

29

ucated but about survival. These stories confirmed the bleak picture Sizer had painted in *Horace's Compromise*. Sizer found that even wealthier, more middle-class, "successful" high schools were large, anonymous factories (even if also often physically attractive and cheerful) focused on everything but learning to use one's mind well. Teachers, he noted sympathetically, faced with 150 or more students daily, had compromised their standards not out of malice but out of necessity. In fact, the stories our graduates told us were generally far worse, with no "shopping-mall campuses" to distract them from the intellectual barrenness. It was hard to avoid the good reasons for trying to create an alternative, at least for our *own* students.

We began negotiations with the district and with the Central Board of Education. We committed ourselves openly and loudly to being different, to keeping alive the ideas and spirit of good early childhood education, and to graduating our students, as Sizer and the newly formed Coalition of Essential Schools recommended, on the basis of publicly accessible "exhibitions." The last idea, now popularly known as performance or portfolio-based graduation, requires our students to prepare tangible demonstrations of their knowledge and competence rather than accumulating "seat-time" (credits) or grades on multiple choice tests. Sizer reminded us that such exhibits had a long and honorable tradition, including bar mitzvahs, Boy Scout rituals, Red Cross tests, and doctoral committees. While experimental colleges had tried something on this order (e.g., the University of Chicago in the 1940s, Hampshire College in the 1970s), we knew of only one other public high school that had done so—Walden II in Wisconsin. We traveled out to see their work and borrowed many of our ideas from them.

In the fall of 1985 we opened with 80 seventh-graders, and thus began Central Park East Secondary School (CPESS). Today it serves 450 seventh- through twelfth-graders, only half of whom ever went to one of our elementary schools. Then it was one of five new schools supported by Ted Sizer's Coalition of Essential Schools nationwide; today it's one of more than seven hundred secondary schools (including several dozen in New York) affiliated with the Coalition. In 1985 it seemed we were back where we began in 1974, launching a new way of thinking about public high schools as we had earlier done in the field of elementary education. But unlike 1974, the 1980s were an auspicious moment for thinking big. As we celebrate the tenth anniversary of CPESS we are part of a major city- and statewide challenge to reshape public education along the lines we've pioneered.

The launching of the high school, however, produced special challenges we had not dealt with before. We began with far less self-confidence. The Central Park East elementary schools benefited from their low profiles. No one demanded proof of our success except us; we weren't seen as a threat, except perhaps to the principals closest to us; we had no visitors or media to contend with, and the privacy, therefore, to make mistakes without fear of exposure. Even though the elementary schools began with skimpy tax-levy budgets and no outside financial support, our limited visibility freed us to take educational risks that most school bureaucrats could never have allowed.

The secondary school, in contrast, has had a high profile from Day One, as have all the Coalition's efforts. We wanted it that way; we thought it worth the risks, which are plenty. In addition, as an official new high school rather than a wildcat District 4 invention, we were entitled to the usual start-up tax-levy support provided to new schools, and we have had some private foundation support for staff development, retreats, consultants, and technology that we neither asked for nor received for our elementary schools. But the obstacles that block the path of reforming a high school are harder to budge than those that face elementary schools. Bureaucratic and financial impediments are only parts of the picture, and not the most difficult ones. The biases and prejudices of the larger society have more obvious effects as youngsters come closer to the "real thing"—being adults. The external demands for proof and evidence are far greater in high school, the rituals more fixed (curriculum, credit hours, course sequences, daily schedules), and the "next" institution—college or workplace—even less under our influence. But even these factors were not the most important.

The big, mindless high school, no matter how dysfunctional,

has many fans, including kids. When we talk with school officials and local politicians about restructuring large high schools, the first thing they worry about is what will happen to the basketball or base-ball teams, the after-school program, and other sideshows; that the heart of the school, its capacity to educate, is missing, seems almost beside the point. Furthermore, we've glorified a teen culture that's out of control and adultless. Kids are accustomed to their "free-dom." At CPESS, new students often find so many caring adults a nuisance—"in my face," as they say. And anxieties about whether the new schemes we are trying will prepare students properly for the "real world" press upon high-schoolers as well as their parents and teachers.

We knew we had to challenge the assumptions behind these high-stakes anxieties especially. Do you change supervisors every forty minutes in the real world? we asked. Not to mention job tasks or team members? In what real-world job is the sequence of tasks (classes) so unconnected to the larger product? What college stu-dent attends eight lecture courses a day running back-to-back with only one short breather? We introduced two-hour interdisciplinary class periods and demanded exhibitions—projects—rather than short-answer written tests. We provided time during those two hours for presentations, seminars, group work, and independent study. We built in time for tutorials and coaching. We insisted that this was more like the real world, not less. But mostly we had to say "Wait and see."

Traditional course requirements, assumptions about college ad-mission policies and SATs, and the usual panic about dealing with adolescents and their hormones combined in those first years to make everyone nervous. We had, in addition, to decide how to re-spond to the New York State Regents' "Action Plan" of 1984, with its increased number of required courses and standardized exami-nations, and its greater specificity about both the sequencing and content of courses. We promised to meet the "spirit" of the new plan, and more, but publicly ignored the mandated route.

But over and over the most serious barrier facing us was the dearth of experience with progressive education at the secondary school level anywhere in the country, even in private or suburban schools that had a tradition of progressive schooling on the elementary level. Our elementary schools had had a plethora of models, experts, and literature. Teacher education programs were available in all the best colleges, staffed by proponents of progressive, child-centered elementary education. This was not the case in secondary education teacher training programs. The better so-called progressive high schools were mostly distinguished by having smaller class sizes, more course choices, more student input, and more intellectually stimulating discourse—goals they achieved mostly by having more money and wealthier students and by accepting only the already self-motivated and successful. A student- and learner-centered curriculum and pedagogy and the commitment to educate all children which are characteristic of progressive elementary education had gotten lost in the translation to high school. We had to invent the translation.

We had to go back to "ancient history" for our lessons, to the bold 1930s experiment known in the field as the Eight-Year Study. Led by school theorist Ralph Tyler, the project was cut short by World War II—although not before "proving" that radical change worked. This fifty-year-old story offered a sobering message: the project had left almost no traces! Resistance to change was deep-rooted, not specific to one community, one set of individuals, particular forms of bad luck. Entrenched practice had a way of creeping back; old habits die hard.

We had a lot going for us, however. We had our three sister elementary schools to lean on and draw support from. We were part of a flexible and inventive alternative high school bureaucracy; we had the support of the fledgling Coalition of Essential Schools, with considerable national status and glamour, and a growing national interest. Not least of all, we were physically located in the one local district that despite political upheavals still supported the idea of "schools of choice." Anthony Alvarado's brief one-year tenure as citywide chancellor was critical, too, as it was Alvarado who initiated the Alternative High School Division, which began the tradition of small secondary schools, albeit at first for those students no one else wanted—the throwaways, dropouts, so-called misfits. It was Alvarado who also gave the green light for Central Park East Secondary School (which was later supported by the Alternative Division). His replacements in District 4, starting with Carlos Medina, mostly maintained the tradition of support for innovation. Medina and his deputy, Sy Fliegel, worked out, for example, the conundrums necessary to clear the road for CPESS to move into a thoroughly discredited and nearly empty junior high. Their creativity enabled us to avoid having to hire a small cadre of burned-out teachers with something known as "building tenure." Instead we were able to hire volunteers who were willing to try something totally untested.

The oddest, or perhaps merely saddest, thing is that the incredible experience of District 4 has taken so long to have any impact on the rest of New York City. It drew attention, but most of the energy of the Central Board of Education (and some quite prolific reporters and school reform networks) went into proving that District 4's elementary school successes were exaggerated (probably true) or that its finances and administrative practices were questionable or at least unorthodox. The bureaucratic resistance was expected; resistance from so many reformers was worrisome. Here and there another district experimented with District 4's innovative practices. But few schools were willing to break decisively with the traditional mold. Officials would proclaim the existence of alternative programs or mini-schools, but made sure they had little real power as separate institutions with their own leadership, space, and budgets. Sometimes the alternatives were only for the "gifted" (often wealthier and whiter) or only for those having trouble with school (darker and poorer). Such mini-schools tended to come and go at the political whim of the district or school supervisor.

Our hope that "next year" our ideas would finally catch on has endured for twenty years. (Of course the ideas themselves are far older.) Perhaps what is surprising is that our approach has now become fashionable, rather than the object of resistance that it was for so long. And perhaps the fact that next year kept moving one year further away suggests that parents and teachers, not just bureaucrats, were for a long time more satisfied with the status quo than reformers understood. Maybe it took the threat of privatization to loosen the hold of old ways.

Our high school experiment, for its part, caught the public's attention and fancy almost immediately. In fact, CPESS was proclaimed a success even before it had any data to show for itself, while CPE's elementary schools were subject to skepticism long after they had demonstrated success. High schools are of course more clearly in a state of crisis. Adolescent students who are in trouble *cause* trouble, unlike their younger counterparts. High school violence scares citizens who might otherwise not care. The high dropout rate (nearly 50 percent in New York City) along with the fate of many of those who do not drop out officially has proven embarrassing and visible. Perhaps these glaring and tangible realities make Dewey's ideas of progressive education seem once again worth looking at after a hiatus of over forty years.

But while there is a rhetorical acceptance, it's an uneasy one, and by no means yet secure. At the heart of the idea of progressive education is a still unaccepted notion: that giving both adolescents and their teachers greater responsibility for the development of their schools can't be by-passed. Without a radical departure from a more authoritarian model, one strips the key parties of the respect which lies at the heart of democratic practice and good schooling. As long as we see "these kids" as dangers to our civil peace and their teachers as time-servers or crazy martyrs, we are not likely to offer either group the respect they need to make schools work. Schools for thoughtfulness can't be built on top of thoughtlessness.

Unfortunately, most of today's urban high schools express *dis*respect for teachers and students in myriad ways—in the physical decay of the buildings, in the structure of the school day, in the anonymity of both students and staff and their lack of control over decisions affecting them. Size alone—say 3,000 students and 200 adults per school—makes staff and student participation in decision making a matter of lip service at best. In many public high schools the average faculty member sees 150 students a day, and every semester the rosters change.

Central Park East Secondary School, like the dozen sister

schools that soon followed suit, broke with this traditional design, following the tradition of the CPE elementary schools in opting to be small so that we could know our colleagues and students well; teachers are rarely responsible for more than 40 students a day and stick with the same students for two years. (If we had it to do over again we'd have been even smaller—with no more than 300 students—so that the entire faculty could more easily meet together to talk things out.) We have clear beliefs about teaching and learning, and control over many of the variables that go into schooling. Only in matters of physical plant are we largely still helpless, although we are able at least to work together to make the best of it.

Since students view the schools as theirs, vandalism is rare and artwork abounds on otherwise cracked walls. Bathrooms are functional; toilet stalls have doors. Physical violence is almost unknown. Like the CPE elementary schools, the secondary school has proven that tailor-made schools, designed by users, *work*. When interviewed later, our high school graduates have had this or that complaint about the way we've prepared them, but the results speak louder even than their words. We don't know what most accounts for their success—actual academic skill, work habits, attitudes, or perhaps just the capacity to relate to adults, to negotiate complexity and independence. We continue to monitor CPESS graduates year by year, as we did our elementary school graduates, and we listen closely to their feedback, both to help us refine what we're doing at the school and to help prepare them for the adjustments they must learn to make.

CPE and CPESS are not meant to be copied piece by piece. The current reform mood offers us an opening, but only if we can resist the desire for a new "one best way," for new cookie-cutter solutions that can be easily "replicated." We will not achieve the reforms we need by fiat. There are top-down mandates that might help, but they are few. One of them—giving more power to those who are closest to the classroom—is not the kind that appeals to busy legislators, politicians, and central board officials. Even teachers' unions (who, like other advocacy and defense organizations, have built top-down structures that mimic "the enemy") have often looked askance at giving teachers more direct influence. In our case, our insistence on placing teachers in the forefront of our reforms, plus the particulars of the local union's leadership, helped pave the way for unprecedented, if often only tacit, support. (The union's secondary leadership remains suspicious as the union begins to openly explore more flexible responses to school-based democracy.)

Not only are our colleagues in other schools wary, our fellow citizens are suspicious, too. Small, democratically run schools are both quintessentially American and hard for Americans to swallow. They appeal to our spirit of independence, but not to our impatient desire for guaranteed fixes and standardized products. In the face of vast school failure, such reforms argue for fewer rules, not more of them. They smack of a kind of trustfulness that a heterogeneous and complex society finds reason to be wary of. Not only are good schools hard to replicate, but they aren't even easily compared to one another! To institutionalize this kind of change process requires not blind faith but a nurturing watchfulness, continuous documenting and recording, and plenty of public exposure.

Do we have the collective will to take such risks? Will enough good examples make a difference? (And how many is enough?) It's hard to convince people that what we do at CPE or CPESS *is* reproducible by others—*in their own way*. People often have a whole string of "well, buts" for why our situation is different from theirs. Principals visit the school and say, Ah, but you have only four hundred students; I could do it too if I had only four hundred. I say, Terrific, you can divide your building into a bunch of smaller schools, as we have. So then they say, Well, you have so much more freedom than I do. I remind them that no one actually gave it to me or to us. We have what we took. They say, You have an unusual staff. I agree, but it's not because they went to more elite colleges, taught longer, or have exceptional gifts. What's unusual is that they are practicing what they believe in and working in settings they design. We've proven that these kinds of schools work over and over again with different directors, with different staffs, and without extra funds. It isn't even a uniquely urban story, as visits to schools throughout the nation remind me. The nearly all-white rural kids at Thayer High School in New Hampshire would fit right in at CPESS. The secret ingredient is wanting it badly enough.

If what we've done is to have wider applicability we need to look upon our story as an example, not a model, and then make it easier—not harder—for others to do similar things in their own way. We need to insist that there cannot be just one right, perfectly crafted, expertly designed solution. Good schools, like good societies and good families, celebrate and cherish diversity. Since we don't know the ending ahead of time, life's unpredictability is a given. After accepting some guiding principles and a firm direction, we must say "hurrah," not "alas," to the fact that there is no single way toward a better future. It's the kind of work that must be done by people who don't all like the same movies, vote for the same politicians, or raise their own kids the same way. It's worth arguing about, leaving room for lots of answers and not being afraid to tell each other the truth.

Dear parents, students and staff

What were you doing in the winter of 1985? Some of us spent that winter "inventing" CPESS. Of course, it's changed a lot since we first invented it, based on ideas from parents, students and new teachers. But also because the best-laid plans never look quite the same when put into practice. But our "habits of mind" probably have held up best of all. (Although we're all inclined to want to add our favorite 6th now and then.)

When we were "inventing" them we settled first on "viewpoint." It's interesting six years later to see how much more difficult the idea is than we anticipated.

In listening to our students defend their work, I realized that many interpreted viewpoint to mean "opinion." They knew that we liked people to have strong opinions and, of course, we hope our school doesn't injure this quality of mind. But it wasn't what we were thinking about.

We probably hit upon "viewpoint" first because in our conversations that winter our different past experiences gave each of us a different way of viewing what we wanted to see happen at CPESS. Planning CPESS required us to articulate our own separate points of view in ways that our colleagues could understand, and then to hear and understand theirs. In the course of this sharing of views I think we built a stronger school.

Recognizing that one's own point of view is just one of many possibilities—that's the first goal I think we had in mind. No two photographers, for example, are ever likely to snap exactly the same picture, if only because no two people are likely to be standing at exactly the same place (at the same time). Photographers have fun with this: creating a whole art of odd but accurate perceptions of reality. No two family members ever see their own family in exactly the same way either.

Where we're coming from as well as what we're up to affects the way we see things. My older brother and I see our family differently because he sees the family from the first-born's perspective. But the two of us may also have different interests that shape what we see and say. It helps to know something about the speaker, writer or artist before judging the meaning of their work. Who is he and what's he up to? Sometimes I can find the evidence right there in the text (or photograph). But sometimes I have to dig a bit to hear the "hidden" voice.

Finally, the hardest task for many may be stepping into the other guy's shoes for a while, long enough to see the world as someone else sees it. Living vicariously through the characters in a novel is something I love. For me, reading novels is an escape from my daily troubles. But sometimes it's tougher, and I resist even a very good book. I think I sometimes resist when it means living inside the mind of someone I'd hate if I met him in real life! Suppose the "hero" is a racist, a sexist, a murderer, a German soldier in World War II? The greater the novel or movie the harder it is to resist, and when I give in I often find I've learned a lot from stepping into some pretty unpleasant shoes! It's good practice for thinking about political issues too.

The more I sit here and write about this, the more complicated it gets! I don't really think we had all this in mind when we started. But a good idea has a natural habit of growing.

CPESS NEWSLETTER

Who Cares & So What

CPESS focuses on five major "intellectual habits"—habits that should be internalized by every student, and used no matter what they are studying about, both in school and especially out of it! These five "habits" include concern for evidence (how do you know that?), viewpoint (who said it and why?), cause and effect (what led to it, what else happened), and hypothesizing (what if, supposing that).

But most important of all is the 5th "habit": who cares? Knowing and learning take on importance only when we are convinced it matters, it makes a difference. Having a good mind and being well-educated don't always seem important at 15 years of age.

It matters because it will help us get ahead, get into a good college, hold a well-paying job.

But that's not the whole story!

It will also help save the world!

That sounds kind of corny. But it's also true.

The song of the Civil Rights movement was called "WE shall overcome." For too many Americans these days the song has been rewritten into "I shall overcome." PERIOD.

It's important to be able to stand alone, to take personal responsibility. But it's also important to learn to work together with others—to collaborate. That means not forgetting our family, our friends and our community as we gain success in life.

However, it also means not letting anyone tell us that we have to fail in school in order to keep our friends.

Teenagers are in a lot of conflict between their ambitions, their compassion for others and their loyalties to family and friends. That's where they need you—their parents. There is no better source of wisdom on these issues.

CPESS NEWSLETTER

January 17

It's the day before our Saturday retreat devoted to graduation standards. I'm nervously checking to be sure our external reviewers (college faculty, teachers from other high schools, and so on) have the material they need. Every student must complete the requirements of fourteen different "portfolio" areas: literature, history, ethics, science, math, media, and so on, and present seven of them to a Graduation Committee for questioning and defense. (The other seven are presented for a more cursory review.) The Graduation Committee has at least two assigned faculty, another adult of the student's choice, and a student. The whole thing is like a series of doctoral orals! It takes at least a year from the time the first set of work is presented until the last is approved. The kids take it very seriously. But ensuring that we have a set of shared and publicly defensible standards takes continual re-examination. We select a sample of items—including videos of Graduation Committee meetings—for staffwide review and then, ultimately, for external review. The "outsiders" review the material ahead of time. They start off by discussing their ratings and reasonings. The ratings are then compared with ours, and then we join together to argue over our rationales! It's a form of assessment that builds standards, examines teaching practice, and raises issues of curriculum—all at one and the same time.

The essence of our notion of standards is this publicness. It's like the old one-room schoolhouse evening performance, where kids got up before the whole community and recited poems, were quizzed on history, and so on. It's like a well-done Bar Mitzvah. There's both showmanship and authenticity to it. It's why we're so hostile to the idea of imposed "standards" via tests. They wouldn't be so dangerous if they were low-stakes exams that were used mostly on a sampled basis or as a way to get a second opinion. But they're being proposed as high-stakes assessments intended to be used to make decisions simultaneously about grade placement, job entry, school accountability, and teacher pay. Snake oil.

And such testing leads to cheating—directly and indirectly. No testing system can ever entirely avoid it. People cheat on eye tests if they need to. I like [our system because] the conversation about the test is part of the test, we're always revising, and the stakes are never too high. They can always try again.

JOURNAL

February 3

Terrific staff meeting on racism. I started off irritated by the session's leader, who had us engage in a bunch of exercises I found silly and embarrassing. I put up with it in what I hope was good grace. Dom and Howie (both white) then role-played a white parent luring a white teacher into a discussion about "those" kids in a clearly racist way. The tension among the white and black teachers was very sharp. Lois (white) felt sure it was a "straw man"; no white parent in our school would be so openly racist. I agreed.

43

Dom said it had actually happened in just this way, and he had responded in just the way he play-acted! I was aghast at both facts. It helped when someone "played" the white teacher and interrupted the attempted complicitous conversation by insisting that "those" kids were hers. There was an almost audible explosion of relief. We spent an hour or more trying it out other ways, while everyone commented and criticized different approaches. A lot of interesting issues surfaced. Would it be any more acceptable in our school if an African-American or Latino teacher did the same thing with a fellow African-American or Latino parent? I tried it out with Sandra (African-American). I played the African-American parent sharing "our" shared perception of whites in the school. I hammed it up but the African-American teachers laughed in recognition. It looked less simple to me when reversed. But lots of staff had trouble with it both ways. I think everyone left feeling intrigued and pleased. I know Sandra gets mad at me for saying that these race/class/gender discussions will only work if they're "fun." All this talk about its being "painful but necessary" is a mistake, I argue. Granted, the African-American staff feel the pain all the time, so why shouldn't we? But pain is not the best educator. Not for kids or adults. The kind of thing we learn best from pain is avoidance and bitterness. (A little "discomfort" is probably okay.) Maybe whites are morally bound to suffer the pain. But so what? Pain works when it's strictly voluntary—when you're in control of the level of pain! But the staff meetings are something else.

I felt vindicated today. We've come a long way. It's getting easier to talk this way together. I came away feeling I'd caught on to something that had seemed elusive before. Is it translating into how we dare talk with kids? Because they desperately need opportunities to sort out racism—to deal with it in a "safe" way. They're as touchy as the staff. Self-doubt and a sense of hopelessness are things you can chip away at. But we're all naturally nervous about exposing ourselves to the underlying rage.

JOURNAL

3 The School at Work

We started Central Park East Secondary School with an important conviction, that expertise in early childhood development is a good foundation for starting a school for adolescents. In fact, we believe such expertise stands us in good stead in educating ourselves as adults, too.

We all have more in common with five-year-olds than we imagine; adults remain, in Piaget's terms, "concrete thinkers," and little kids, lo and behold, are capable of some very fancy abstractions. Think about how deeply we've accepted the notion that young students lack "attention spans" because they're "immature," when in fact it's small children who have the longest and most tenacious attention spans. (Watch an infant struggling for half an hour to work out some new theory of how an object moves from one place to another.) It's boredom and anxiety that drive concentration away; fidgetiness appears in first grade and grows worse over time.

Just as our elementary school was based on the idea of keeping the traditions of kindergarten going through the sixth grade, so for our secondary school we largely imagined our task as keeping the spirit of kindergarten going for a few more years. I do not mean this to sound condescending or belittling. I see the spirit I'm referring to as fundamental to all good education; wouldn't it be wonderful, after all, if high school students were as deeply absorbed in their "work" as five-year-olds are in their "play"?

47

I entered teaching accidentally and became a kindergarten teacher because it was convenient; the work was available part-time and across the street from my house. I didn't have any intention of becoming a teacher, much less a teacher of little children. And there I was doing both. This fortuitous opportunity to work with young children gave me a particular viewpoint and perspective that has, as much as anything else, shaped all my subsequent efforts. I have carried a kindergarten teacher's perspective with me, first into elementary school and now into high school.

Kindergarten is the one place—maybe the last place—where teachers are expected to know children well, even if they don't hand in their homework, finish their Friday tests, or pay attention. Kindergarten teachers know children by listening and looking. They know that learning must be personalized because kids are incorrigibly idiosyncratic. (I speak here of an old-fashioned kindergarten, one that doesn't look like a first grade.) Kindergarten teachers know that helping children learn to become more self-reliant is part of their task—starting with tying shoes and going to the bathroom. Catering to children's growing independence is a natural part of a kindergarten teacher's classroom life. This is, alas, the last time children are given independence, encouraged to make choices, and allowed to move about on their own steam. The older they get the less we take into account the importance of children's own interests, and the less we cherish their capacity for engaging in imaginative play. (In fact, we worry in kindergarten if children lack such capacity, while later on we worry if they show it too much.) In kindergarten we design our rooms for real work, not just passive listening. We put things in the room that will appeal to children, grab their interests, and engage their minds and hearts. Teachers in kindergarten are editors, critics, cheerleaders, and caretakers, not just lecturers or deliverers of instruction. What Ted Sizer calls "coaching" is second nature in the kindergarten classroom.

A good school for anyone is a little like kindergarten and a little like a good post-graduate program—the two ends of the educational spectrum, at which we understand that we cannot treat any two human beings identically, but must take into account their special interests and styles even as we hold all to high and rigorous standards. A good Oxford education is more like my kindergarten classroom than it is like the typical American high school or public college. We don't need research on this astounding proposition. The main difference between the advantaged and the disadvantaged is that the latter need such flexible schools even more. When people think "those kids" need something special, the reply we offer at CPESS is, Just give them what you have always offered those who have the money to buy the best, which is mostly a matter of respect.

I think we've created a framework at CPESS for creating such a respectful setting, day by day. We don't create all the conditions that affect our students' lives; we can't stop the world our students live in while we do our work, a world that places crushing burdens on far too many of our young people. We have no guarantees to offer our kids, their families, or the wider public beyond trying our best to make CPESS a place that at least temporarily makes life seem more interesting and more worth the effort.

For this to happen, teachers first need a framework that enables them to know their students as learners well. This takes time and trust. Trust can't be mandated, but because students and families come to us by choice, at least some modest basis for mutual trust is built in—at least choice buys us time. Teachers also need to know— or decide—what they can expect of each other. They need to agree not only on what to teach, but also on how their teaching and their kids' learning will be assessed. We refuse to let our work be judged on the basis of a students' capacity to collect trivia. We want it to be judged instead on the intellectual habits of mind it engenders. And we also value certain habits of work: the acceptance of increasing levels of responsibility, the increasing capacity to communicate appropriately to others, a willingness to take a stand as well as a willingness to change one's mind, and being someone who can be counted on to meet deadlines as well as keep one's word.

We threw together the "CPESS Habits of Mind" in a hurry as we realized the need to create a unity across disciplines and a focus on the essential that hadn't seemed so critical in the younger grades. It was all very well to refer to "habits of mind," but the phrase seemed too abstract. We didn't want an endless laundry list either, so we wrote down five, based on many years of watching kids and observing our own habits, and now they are posted in most classrooms and appear regularly in our weekly newsletter. They are at the heart of each curriculum as well as being the basis for judging student performance. We have, on occasion, played around with adding a sixth or replacing one with something different, if only to remind ourselves and the world that they weren't handed to us from Above. We never quite write them out the exact same way, and over the years we've realized they are constantly evolving in their meaning. They are: the question of evidence, or "How do we know what we know?"; the question of viewpoint in all its multiplicity, or "Who's speaking?"; the search for connections and patterns, or "What causes what?"; supposition, or "How might things have been different?"; and finally, why any of it matters, or "Who cares?"

Lawyers tell us these "habits" are very lawyerly, but journalists and scientists tell us they are basic to what they do as well. As a historian I recognize them as being at the heart of my field. As a principal I find them useful when "naughty" kids are sent to my office. I ask them to put their version of the story on one side and that of whoever sent them to me on the other, then we consider evidence that corroborates either version, discuss whether what's happened is part of a pattern, how else it might have been dealt with, and, finally, why it matters.

In order to make such "habits" habitual, they need in-depth practice. Young people need to be immersed in their use. We want to demand evidence in the form of performance at real, worthwhile tasks. To do this we devote ourselves to covering less material, not more, and to developing standards that are no less tough and no less rigorous than those associated with traditional displays of academic excellence but sometimes different. It's very hard to use these habits in the typical survey course, no matter how provocatively taught. As we rush through a hundred years of history in less than a week, or cover complex new scientific ideas one after another, there's no time to study conflicting evidence, read multiple viewpoints, detect the difference between false analogies and real ones, not to mention imagine how else it might have happened. The first time I really did these things as a student was in graduate school in a course on the French Revolution. It was the first time I understood what history meant; that the history of the world was at least as complicated as my own family's story (and certainly my brother and I have a hard time agreeing on a single version of that).

As teachers, we see the habit of asking these kinds of questions as critical to our students' education not because our kids have special disadvantages, but because it's what we want for all children. But building standards based on these habits of mind takes time, takes translating back and forth between theory and practice, between our ideas and samples of real student work. Can a student do a distinguished piece of work at CPESS without demonstrating breadth of knowledge about the larger context? Is it okay if Francis knows a lot about Japan's involvement in World War II and uses diverse sources with considerable discrimination but seems to know very little about the same war in Europe? Is it okay to be comfortable with ideas and experimental evidence in the field of genetics but superficially ignorant about a presumably simpler phenomenon like photosynthesis? Teaching this way requires forms of rigor few of us have ever before demanded of ourselves. It doesn't mean dispensing with all shallower "survey" requirements, but it shifts the balance dramatically. And it creates anxiety as we ask, But what will other people say if our kids don't know x or y? Of course, in reality their peers who take the traditional courses don't remember x or y anyway. But while that's reassuring, it's a cop-out. So it's an endless tension, a see-sawing back and forth between "coverage" and making sense of things.

The resolution of such weighty issues won't matter in the end if we don't simultaneously deal with the relationship of the school to our students' communities and families. Respect among children's families, their community, and the school is an end in itself, as well as an essential means to the education we have in mind. It isn't merely a question of good and frequent contact between school and family. That's hard enough, but it takes more. The gap between the social, ethnic, and class histories of the school's staff and the school's families is often substantial. Even with the best of intentions, none of our schools have a majority of African-American and Latino teachers on their faculties, and few of our teachers grew up in East Harlem or neighborhoods like it. It's a gap we cannot bridge by good intentions alone. There's a price to be paid. At minimum, parents need to know that we will do our best not to undermine their authority, their values, or their standards, although we will encourage our students to raise questions about them. We don't demand that Seventh-Day Adventists accept our scientific version of the world's origins, but we require that they explore this view with us. We acknowledge the existence of different ways of handling conflict, but we insist that they use our way in school. We can't do away with the likelihood that some of our students' families see white teachers as inherently suspect, but white teachers can listen, we can reconsider our own reactions, offer alternative possibilities, and challenge some implicit assumptions.

We know that the school's pedagogy doesn't always rest easily with parents, some of whom wonder if we're not creating difficulties for children already handicapped by racism or poverty. We're not always going to be convincing, but we need to provide evidence that where we disagree we do so respectfully, that we're not out to frustrate the aspirations parents have for their kids, or to blame them for what goes wrong. Children must take increasing responsibility for who they are and what they accomplish, which includes sorting out the unresolved tensions between school and family. At their best, family and school are allies, however cautiously, but the kid is the performer. Adolescence is a time of experimentation, and we want our students to take on new challenges, to look at the world and their own life histories in novel ways. These two ideas—a commitment to avoid fostering an alienation between students and their families and a commitment to opening new doors and pathways for them—don't always rest easily together. In the end however, CPE and CPESS are more often faulted by kids for being too close, not too distant, from their families and community. It's amazing how much can be done to bridge the gaps if we eliminate some of the obvious barriers.

When school people complain that parents "these days" don't show up at parent/teacher conferences, especially in high schools, I remember my own experiences as a parent attending school conferences. At best, the teachers restated what I already knew: my child was doing fine or he or she wasn't. Bad news at the conference was more than useless. I left such meetings feeling more inadequate, more guilty, and more helpless. I learned to stop going. It was an act of intelligence and survival, not a lack of concern, that led me to stay away. Such avoidance can produce distrust and wariness, and our children sometimes pay a paralyzing price. Children can get stuck between the two suspicious, warring parties to their education even if no confrontation ever takes place.

One obvious way of maintaining a climate that favors trust is by running a small rather than a large school. In many public schools across the country anything under 2,000 is thought of as tiny, hardly a school at all. We feel our high school enrollment of 450 is actually too big. It requires more subdivisions than is ideal. Incidentally, all 450 kids can fit into our auditorium, which is one criterion for maximum size. The other useful criterion is whether or not the entire staff can meet face to face, preferably in a single circle.

Experts at team building claim a group works best at somewhere between 15 and 20 people. By this standard, both class size and staff size should top at around 20. Having miscalculated a little on size, we divided the school into three major divisions, each with about 150 kids and 8 or 9 primary adults covering nearly all subjects taught, along with a "resource" teacher with a specialty in learning disabilities. The divisions are further subdivided each into two houses of 75 to 80 students, each with its own core faculty of 4. Most teachers are responsible for more than a single discipline, so we can combine courses such as math and science. This reduces the number of students a teacher deals with by half. We've also cut administrators, supervisors, and some specialists.

Thus, with the same budget as the typical city school we've cut the number of children a teacher sees each day from 160 to only 40. More like an elementary school. The 40 includes a group of about 15 students that each teacher sees daily for an extended advisory period—a combination tutorial, seminar, and study hall—and whose families the adviser keeps informed about how things are going. (All professional staff—principal, social worker, librarian, special ed staff—run advisory groups as well.) This means that on parent/teacher evenings each staff member has only 15 families to meet with. Quite a different task than the one that faced my son's high school teachers. Parents have the opportunity to talk with someone who actually knows their son or daughter! The talk lasts at least half an hour, and both the student and the student's work are there as well. It takes time: several evenings, one afternoon, and some early mornings to reach everyone. A simple idea, but one that the average urban high school can't pretend to hold itself to.

Students spend two years in each division at CPESS, and with the same adviser. Division I is the equivalent of grades 7 and 8, and Division II consists of grades 9 and 10. Students remain in the last division, called the Senior Institute, as long as they need to get a diploma and be prepared for the next step in their lives. Within each division no distinctions are made by grade level; everyone studies the same broad subject matter together, and it's easy for us to forget who is in what grade. But the kids seem to know. Since we avoid holdovers in the earlier grades, there are a number of students who need more time at the end. Students who spend a third year in the Senior Institute work with their advisers more independently, often taking off-campus courses, maybe working part-time, doing more independent study, and progressing as fast as they can toward completion of the required portfolios. Kids still feel strongly about graduating with "their class"; despite our efforts to fudge over these categories, spending that extra time is hard. For a few it doesn't work, but most proudly show up at graduation the following June to receive their diplomas, and one or two have come back for their diplomas a year or more later! The kids think a CPESS diploma is special.

"Keep the schedule simple, so you can focus on the complexity of the kids and the complexity of the ideas they are dealing with," Sizer recommended when we began. So we did. We kept it as close to our elementary school schedule as we dared. We decided on the simplest of schedules: two hours each day in Humanities (art, history, literature, social studies), two hours daily of Math and Science, and one hour of Advisory. That's the routine, day after day, with almost no change for the first four years, from grades 7 through 10. Some kids attend Humanities first, while the others have Math/Science; then it reverses. Within each two-hour block, the staff makes decisions about time and grouping. They can decide to do one thing on Monday and change their minds on Tuesday. They can even quickly decide to spend one whole day on Science! When the kids and teachers complained once that no one seemed really prepared to study hard after lunch, we all grumbled about it until the kids suggested a simple solution: no after lunch. So we run four hours straight three days a week, eat lunch late, and put Advisory at the end of the day. Everyone prefers it, at least for now. This was a decision we were able to make on Monday and put into effect within the same week. In most New York high schools, it would take a task force months to study an idea like this and more months or years to put it into effect. We just sat in our circle, listened to the kids' proposal and said, Let's try it.

One morning per week each student in grades 7 through 10 spends in community service, which allows for teacher planning time. Also, between 8:00 and 9:00 each morning we offer foreign language—with a mostly auxiliary staff of language teachers. The kids think 8:00 A.M. is outrageously early and they are still giving us a hard time about promptness. But being on time is a necessity for our kind of schedule, so we aren't budging. Our policy at present is based on theater time: if you arrive late you have to wait for a scheduled intermission. (It's somewhat different once you get into the Senior Institute, where students take some courses off campus, are involved in an extended internship at some point, and have a wider selection of mostly one-hour classes.)

We also have an hour for lunch, longer than is typical. This gives the staff time together, and it gives the students time to eat, choose options such as sports or computers, or use the library for independent study or reading or the wide range of modern technology and media facilities located there. Finally, from 3:00 to 5:00 P.M. and on

Saturday mornings the building is open for interscholastic sports programs, study, homework, or tutoring in the well-staffed library, and for a few student or staff-initiated clubs. Between 4:00 and 5:00 P.M. kids and staff are still hanging around, in and out of classes and offices, often together. This kind of schedule is not only simple, it also provides time—six scheduled school hours a week—for faculty to meet and talk to each other, to do collegially what people who work together need to do.

To create a staff-run school with high standards, the staff must know each other well, too, be familiar with each other's work, and know how the school operates. Each team of teachers that works with the same students and the same curriculum also teaches at the same time and are "off" together. The school's structure, from the placement of rooms to the scheduling of the day, is organized to enable teachers to visit each other's classes, to reflect on their own and their colleagues' practice, and give each other feedback and support. Curricular teams who teach the same division of students the same agreed-upon topics, for example, have a full morning each week outside the classroom to critique student work and each other's plans, and occasional full days to work on standards and long-range expectations. For the same reason, those who teach the same eighty kids—the faculty of each house—have an hour-and-a-half extended lunch together every week. The entire staff meets from 3:00 to 5:00 P.M. every Monday and from 1:30 to 3:00 P.M. on Fridays to make collective schoolwide decisions, discuss ideas, and work out both curricular and graduation standards, issues that overlap all ages and divisions. The staff is responsible for hiring their own members, assessing their own colleagues, and when dissatisfied for confronting colleagues with their concerns. They are responsible for developing and assessing both the curriculum and their students' success with it. Above all, the teachers are responsible for defining, and defending, the criteria for receiving a CPESS diploma. All faculty sit on senior graduation committees. Each potential graduate's name comes before the full faculty, who must vote to give them a diploma based on work presented and publicly accessible.

This structure took time to develop and there are plenty of still unresolved issues in the way our school works. How do we know if we've developed sufficiently high standards for graduation? We have created a system of regular external reviews by panels of experts consisting of college faculty, high school colleagues, parents, community leaders, discipline experts, and educational policymakers and officials. It's effective but probably too cumbersome as presently constituted, especially if many schools were to adopt it. Can technology solve any of this for us? What does it mean to tell kids the content of their final exam at the beginning of a course as the Coalition of Essential Schools' "planning backward" strategies suggest? Can one really design final "essential questions" so craftily that answering them requires a student to deal with the curriculum in a serious and systematic way? So far it seems easier said than done, particularly in math and science. How much should each teacher's curriculum and pedagogy be the result of team decision making rather than individual inclination? Unlike our CPE elementary schools, where teachers select topics with extraordinary freedom based on personal inclination and professional judgments, teams (and ultimately the whole faculty) make such decisions in the secondary school. While both the elementary and high school faculties accept responsibility for all students, there is more built-in joint decision making on the secondary level. If this is a good idea, should we do more of it on the elementary level?

Unresolved also is our effort to deal with racism. No school in America can avoid the issue, but it's self-evident in a place like CPE. This means that dealing with such questions among ourselves as staff—honestly and yet carefully—has to happen alongside of our work with kids. How can we ensure that we don't tear the school apart as we pick our way through such thorny underbrush? There's no pretending that we don't need to do this, or that once we clear it all up we can get on to other things. We must deal with this issue over and over if we are to help kids who desperately need to be able to talk with adults about such difficult matters, and must do so long before

57

we have "solved" them. We need to take chances even though making mistakes can be dangerous. We've called in outside experts on racism as well as experts on group relations to work with us on both a regular basis and in times of crisis, when these issues seemed likely to split us apart. A bitter charge by some parents that a white teacher was not only a racist but out to injure children of color, and the overtones of anti-Semitism that went with it, didn't produce the same instinctive response in all of us. We didn't reach a consensus, except on how to get through it safely. Acknowledging the depth of harm that racism has caused and yet not allowing it to be an excuse for expecting less of our kids or the school, always plagues us, our students, and their families. Every family conference or student conflict with a peer or a teacher can potentially raise issues of race. These can be excuses or they can be fundamental roadblocks. It's not easy to know when to open up the topic and when to leave it closed. The very mention of race can be misinterpreted. But it's not the only super-charged issue. Gender issues for a school full of adolescents are also powerful. And class is even more taboo. The kids are super-sensitive to any hint of a put-down, like being called "disadvantaged," even by reporters who mean to praise them or the school.

And there is never enough time to work any of these issues through! So we look, usually unsuccessfully, for shortcuts. In a school with a faculty of thirty rather than twelve, face-to-face democratic school governance often seems impossible. What role can a smaller cabinet play? What is the role of inexperienced novices compared to that of the more experienced staff? What are the limits on a faculty's legitimate right to make decisions versus the necessary controls exercised by a community, school board, principal, or parent organization? In what capacity and by what means should students play a role in governing their own schools?

These are just a few of our unresolved issues. Most will never be finally resolved. But as we struggle with them we've seen dramatic changes. Because our adult debates are not hidden from our students, there is no sharp dividing line between "staff development" activities and student educational activities. The deep immersion in a value system that places mutual respect first and encourages a climate of diversity and disagreement becomes enormously powerful over time, and not just for the staff. The kids know we're serious. It rubs off. Sometimes we fear that they are just parroting our ideas, but mostly we can't help but be impressed. They are less engaged in battling with us over every imposed limit on their freedom than they once were, and more engaged with us in the battle to become well educated. They get down to business faster and are more cheerful about more things. They read and write a lot. They talk a lot about their own learning and schooling. They are more self-consciously reflective about how they go about it. Yes, it's partly glibness, but even that glibness is a triumph.

We're happy but not surprised when alumna Lindsay reports from Cornell that our "habits of mind" language really impresses the college faculty, and we glow to hear Erran, Division I terror and self-proclaimed tough guy, talking about evidence and viewpoint and alternative possibilities as he heads off to an Ivy League college.

It's hardly surprising that our rate of retention is very high, that only about 5 percent of our students move or transfer annually. CPESS is a nice place to spend the day and kids willingly travel across the city to stay at CPESS. Attendance is also extraordinarily high; kids and parents show up at family conferences to complain about things to our faces and risk the necessary confrontations. Violence is rare and incidents we consider serious are probably barely noticed in many large urban high schools. The children are willing to let us catch them acting like nice young people who want to be smart. By tenth grade they say "I'm bored" a bit less and admit to being interested in the idea of becoming truly well-rounded citizens a bit more. (And their boredom, after all, isn't all feigned; it sometimes requires us to reconsider what we're doing.)

When they enter the last phase—our Senior Institute—students take on the task of completing fourteen portfolios full of work, including seven major presentations in such areas as math, science, literature, history, the arts, community service and apprenticeship, and autobiography. These "presentations," made to a graduation committee consisting of at least two faculty members, an adult of the student's choice, and another student, are carried out with enormous seriousness and zeal. They are the primary record—transcript—of a student's success at CPESS, and the basis for receiving the diploma. The Saturday morning school was the outgrowth of Senior Institute students' insistence on more time to prepare. They prep each other before, and debrief each other after, each presentation. Committee meetings, originally designed to last about thirty minutes per portfolio, rarely get finished in less than an hour. Starting in seventh grade, kids know what awaits them at the end and have the opportunity to practice this final process each semester as they move through the school and sit through a half-dozen or more meetings as student members of graduation committees. This process, which has its trade-offs in terms of the time required for faculty participation, creates a series of tasks that require a wide range of performance skills, habits of work as well as mind: the sheer ability to put the material together for their committee to review, to arrange and schedule meetings, to make oral presentations and answer unexpected questions with poise and aplomb!

It also means that early on they must tackle the most important question of all—what's this all for? What comes next? Each student's post-graduation plan is the first of the fourteen portfolios, the centerpiece of the Senior Institute and the graduation process, the tool that promises to become the most powerful focuser as we learn to use it better. Creating this plan—a joint activity of student, family and adviser—enables us to put together a package of courses (both on and off campus), internships or apprenticeships, independent study, and other external experiences that will lead a student from the protective cocoon of CPESS's Division II to his or her next and more independent task as a graduate. The entire process of the Senior Institute, from the creation of the first post-graduation plan to the completion of the fourteenth portfolio, brings together our commitment to a personalized education and our commitment to high standards for all—standards we take full public responsibility for stating and defending in ways that all can understand.

The facts that reinforce my confidence that we're on the right track go beyond the statistics. Recently I dropped in on the ninth- and tenth-graders as they were presenting their scenes from *Macbeth* in the school auditorium. They had spent many months working over their ideas about the play, and now they were presenting these ideas to each other. The keen sense of ownership they displayed over the material was astounding to me. It was the product of the kind of leisurely pacing only a school like ours can afford, and they were able to show it off to each other without fear of being ridiculed. They knew that the laughter from the audience was the laughter of colleagues working with not against them. It was a wonderful few hours.

Another confirmation came under less happy circumstances. The infamous so-called wilding assault on a Central Park jogger occurred just a few blocks from our building. That event had a particularly powerful impact on the sensitivities of East Harlem residents. As I came to school after the four-day holiday during which the assault occurred, I knew one thing: we needed time to work out how to deal with the youngsters' reactions. The staff met at lunch to talk about what the kids were saying and how we might respond.

We knew we had to address not only the children's reactions, but also our own fears and angers. We had to face our different responses and learn from them. We also had to help the kids deal with a hungry press, and prevent their unwitting exploitation as cameras, microphones, and reporters with pencils and pads pushed into their lives in order to get firsthand "reactions." The events unfolded in such a way that adolescents in East Harlem were perceived as a threat to decent white middle-class joggers. It was easy for kids to fall into the trap set up by reporters and the general climate and respond as though they were defending the alleged attackers and distancing themselves from the victim. Reorganizing to deal with these issues would not have been possible in a typical New York City high school. Our size, our simple and flexible schedule, the advisory system, and our collegial organization made it feasible to address the crisis together and immediately. The kids as a result felt less exploited, had time to sort out their own feelings and develop their own language for describing them. They also learned that they need not answer reporters at all. It helped them avoid feeling like help-less objects of the prurient interest of the reporters, to be more "in control of the script."

They have such opportunities often as crises hit their world, from the death of a fellow student to the events surrounding the Rodney King trial. On the Friday morning following the Los Angeles riots, we were scheduled for a visit from an all-white Michigan high school chorus, who were coming to sing for us. We on the school's staff were nervous about rumors that some of the week's tension and anger might be directed against these frightened out-of-towners—some students, the rumors claimed, wanted a symbolic protest, a walkout to show their distress. After a few introductory greetings before the packed auditorium, just as we could feel a crisis coming, sixteen-year-old Mark walked resolutely onto the stage. "There are no enemies of ours in this room," he announced, and to resounding applause brought us all together.

Above all a school structure such as ours works for the small crises—rumors of a fight or drug use, family crises and homeless-ness, runaways and attempted suicides, pregnancies and births. We can take the time (the endless hours, it often seems) to attend. Some years ago one of the most beloved members of our larger school community, Josie Hernandez, died. Her children were among our first elementary school graduates, fifteen years before, and one has since returned as a teacher. Ms. Hernandez had become secretary at one of our elementary schools. In short, she mattered to us all in many different ways. Her death could not go by unnoted. We stopped to take stock of her life and its meaning personally and in-dividually. We had to be sure that those students who had known her could attend her memorial service. We had to pay attention to details, not just good intentions.

We can do such things not because we are more caring than other teachers or other schools. Not at all. It's because we have a structure and style that enables us to show our care effectively. What could a high school principal with four thousand students possibly do in the face of such a situation? In such schools a death a day is commonplace, and to take cognizance of individual tragedies would be to lapse into a state of perpetual grief and mourning. The distancing and numbing required in most schools is a fact of life, a necessary coping strategy.

If we want children to be caring and compassionate, then we must provide a place for growing up in which effective care is feasible. Creating such intimate schools is possible even in an existing system of large buildings if we create smaller communities within them. That's what I think the visitors who come to our schools recognize and acknowledge. That is what is visibly obvious.

Caring and compassion are not soft, mushy goals. They are part of the hard core of subjects we are responsible for teaching. Informed and skillful care is learned. Caring is as much cognitive as affective. The capacity to see the world as others might is central to unsentimental compassion and at the root of both intellectual skepticism and empathy. "Any human being sufficiently motivated can fully possess another culture, no matter how 'alien' it may appear to be," argues noted African-American author and literary critic Henry Louis Gates. "But there is no tolerance without respect—and no respect without knowledge." Such empathetic qualities are precisely the habits of mind that require deliberate cultivation—that is, schooling. If such habits are central to democratic life, our schools must become places that cultivate, consciously and rigorously, these moral and intellectual fundamentals.

Moving on to high school has helped us at Central Park East to see where the qualities of a good kindergarten classroom need reinforcement. The imaginative play that we so early abandon, the attention to children's nascent friendships, these are after all merely the precursors of what Piaget called intellectual "decentering," that is, the ability to imagine the world without oneself at its center. As we stint on one we injure the other. As we eliminate from our schools and from children's after-school lives the time and space for exercising their creative imagination and building personal ties, we've cheated our children and our society in a far more critical way than we're inclined to understand.

Are We the Latest Fad?

Sometimes it seems that way. We're not used to being quite so popular at CPE!

Every report, task force, and study being conducted these days comes out with a set of recommendations that sound like a description of CPE and CPESS.

1. Schools should be small and highly personal. Where schools are large they should be broken into interdisciplinary houses.

2. Cooperative learning is a key to successful learning.

3. There should be integration of curriculum: history and literature, math and science, etc.

4. Academic periods should be longer in high schools—at least an hour, ideally two hours.

5. High school homerooms should be full-length periods and serve as serious advisory places, and teachers should stay with the same homeroom for two years or more.

6. Fewer subjects, taught thoroughly, are better than lots of courses taught superficially.

7. Decisions about curriculum, pedagogy and scheduling should be made by on-site professionals.

8. Parents should be informed and involved in their children's education.

9. Students should be expected to demonstrate their abilities directly—to "show" what they know and can do. Multiple-choice tests are not a substitute for the real performance.

10. Students should be expected to engage in socially useful work, and should learn about the world-of-work through school-directed work experiences.

I could go on and on and on! I think of ourselves as having

"pioneered" Conflict Resolution, only to discover that it's now on every educator's list of "must do's." CPE has been insisting on writer's journals for 15 years, and now everyone says it's the thing to do. We've been opponents of basal readers and against reliance on textbooks for 15 years. Now that's the fashionable viewpoint.

I'm so accustomed to swimming against the stream that I'm getting worried.

That's not entirely a joke, folks. We need to be careful that these good ideas don't become just another passing fad. That can happen if *we* become smug, and pretend that the label is the same as the real thing, or that having good intentions is enough.

CPESS NEWSLETTER

4 Myths, Lies, and Other Dangers

The story of Central Park East is important because it offers a chance to shed the mystery and join the challenge of educating all our kids in unprecedented ways. While any good story is idiosyncratic, CPE's story suggests that good universal public education is not an impossible dream—that, as Vito Perrone noted at our school's tenth anniversary, "to dichotomize equity and quality . . . is a massive abuse" of truth.

But for too many people it does seem impossible, even possibly undesirable, to demand both equity and quality. In an era of post–Cold War faith that the marketplace solves problems that governments can't, public schools across the nation are on the defensive. They appear self-evidently bureaucratic, statist, and monopolistic. They are under heavy attack not only for failing to teach basic skills and "higher-order" thinking, but also for failing to teach any specific social or moral values *and* for teaching too many of them. As schools uneasily seek to combine secularism with clear personal and civic norms they threaten many and please few. And on top of that, we're told that their shared failings have caused a crisis in the American economy and thus the American way of life.

Citizens grumble helplessly about the mess our schools are in and revert to old and often contradictory bromides for fixing them. The discussion is sour and pessimistic. We're simultaneously committed to producing equitable outcomes and to being sure that the "have-nots" don't hold back the "haves," that the rank order remains intact. There is no public language for high hopes for all, but there is a lot of mean-spirited anger at those responsible for "today's youth," alongside of highly abstracted employer-driven hype about "schools for the twenty-first century." Meanwhile parents are left with deep anxiety that everyone is worrying about "other people's kids" and no one is attending to theirs.

Only on the radical right is there much steam, however misguided, about schooling in all its real-life detail. The defenders of public education are timid and uncertain by comparison. It's as though they've abdicated responsibility for improving public education to narrow professional and policymaking circles; they go along hoping the experts know best but without much confidence in the likely success of the experts and a lot of doubts about their prescriptions. They may not join the radical right, but they vote down bond issues, complain about spending money on frills they either didn't have in their day or believe we can simply no longer afford in today's "down-sized" economy. Most citizens go along apathetically with whatever latest technocratic solutions are offered—more centralized curriculum and testing, for example. But they do so without much hope that the problem will get better by pushing the right button. They mostly wish everyone would just shape up and do "better." The mainstream—right to left—ritually accepts the current call for change, but high expectations without real hope is a recipe for cynicism.

What are the sources of this prolonged cynicism and disillusionment? Why is there so little enthusiasm for the regenerative power of public life? The answer lies in large part in a false version of reality the nation has bought for too long. Unless we reverse this climate of myths and lies, supporters of public education can't take it for granted that the American love affair with education will necessarily carry with it an acceptance of *public* schooling. The opposition—which calls for privatizing—is strong and mobilized. The defense is not.

On Myths and Lies

The central myth, one causing serious mischief, is the notion that in the past public schools taught more effectively and children learned more thoroughly. It's a given part of almost every conversation about schools and undermines every effort to understand what is wrong and thus what must be righted. The universally accepted story of a system "in decline," of the puzzling inability of a once strong system to do what it once did so well, would make disillusionment reasonable—if it were true. It's not. And this myth of the past, in turn, props up some equally pernicious myths about what most schools are really like today. These distortions prevent citizens from recognizing the real continuities between past and present, which would allow them to do more than just gripe. The good news is that this can be changed with large doses of truth.

Some amazing truths: Until World War II the average American did not graduate from high school. Most teenagers were expected to leave school for unskilled or semiskilled work; even many highly skilled jobs could be aspired to without a high school diploma. On the eve of World War II, the average American had attended school for only nine years, and 12 percent had attended for fewer than five. Only somewhere between 10 and 20 percent of teenagers in most Southern communities were in school at all, a fact that hit black teens the hardest. The term "dropout" is new—most kids hadn't "dropped in" before the 1940s. A substantial minority of high school students in New York City were unashamedly labeled "subnormal." And this was long before special education laws required accepting all youngsters. Even the so-called normal were not given an academic curriculum. The demanding academic track was reserved for those deemed "talented" and bound for college. The vast majority of employers saw precious little about school learning that was essential to the work they needed done. Factory work might take skill, but not the kind of skill academic preparation would enhance. At best school attendance was a mark of diligence, which employers did have reason to value. A diploma stood for dutifulness, not academic achievement, in the "good old days."

The cultivation of scholarship and critical thinking, and the development of sophisticated math and science skills, were possibilities for only a few. And even those few were often poorly prepared by today's standards. In the 1940s, even elite, "talented" students rarely took more than two years of high school math, science, or history, and virtually none took calculus—an exclusively college course in those days but today a staple of moderately advanced high school seniors. Latin, not math or science, was the mark of the elite. In New York City, a high school diploma required only one year of science and a year and a half of history and social studies. The truth concerning what students "used to know" about history and science defies the casual conversational litany—heard today on both the right and the left—concerning our ignorant youth. A study published by Dale Whittington in the *American Educational Research Journal* in the winter of 1991 compared the performance of seventeen-year-olds in 1917, 1933, 1944, 1967, and 1987 on test questions concerning the names of U.S. presidents, the dates of wars, the laws of science, and other basic information. The study showed little change over the past seventy years. And what's more, the students tested in those earlier tests represented overall a far more select and elite group than today's general student body; the low performers had mostly already left the school system.

Such hard data is so astounding that few find it believable. Attempts to bring these realities to light are generally hushed up, as though they were a threat to our resolve to undertake tough reforms. Researchers in an eminently respectable federal study released in 1993 by the Sandia National Laboratories were startled to conclude after two years of research that "on nearly every measure we found steady or slightly improving trends" over the past three decades. Not only were these findings not heralded, but the report was, in fact, suppressed, and educational writers like Gerald Bracey were criticized for relentlessly publicizing them. This was in part a response of disbelief; the good news just couldn't be true. A lie told often enough—by such a wide range of different presumably neutral experts or politicians with different axes to grind—gains credibility that withstands mere conflicting evidence.

False history thrives because our memories play tricks on us. We forget, for example, that discipline, gangs, truancy, low standards, social promotion, and plenty of other issues plagued us in the 1930s, 1940s, 1950s, 1960s, and 1970s. *Why Johnny Can't Read* was a bestseller forty years ago. Laura Ingalls Wilder described unruly country boys who thought reading was unmanly a century ago. We've complained about student ignorance, the absence of academic rigor, and the low attainment of our teachers, and parental neglect generation after generation (and probably justly) without noticing that it's never been different. Once history is acknowledged the task may seem even bigger and together, but it will not lend itself to the easy placing of blame, as though we need only recycle the past.

Nostalgia as History

In fact, it was not until the 1960s—just yesterday—that the nation first acknowledged an obligation to educate all students to equally high standards, both because it was fair and because our nation's health depended on it. This rhetorical commitment was not just to making education available to those who proved worthy, but to producing well-educated young people. But rather than accept the idea that educating all children well was a task as complex as going to the moon, that it would require enormous financial resources as well as a revolution in the way we organized teaching and learning, the nation quickly turned its back. As Jonathan Kozol reminds us in *Savage Inequalities*, America in the 1960s created a revolution of rising expectations among those most in need while depriving them of precisely those resources offered those least in need. To rationalize we told ourselves lies. Our penchant for denying that America's educational history is fundamentally elitist has made it easier to argue that old levels of spending and old approaches to schools should be adequate to our present educational expectations—an argument we would recognize as silly if applied to the challenge to travel in space.

It was easier to decide that if kids aren't measuring up it's their fault, not ours. What was good enough for us should be good enough now for "them"; no one, after all, ever coddled *us* when *we* were stupid in school. Yesterday's forgotten lower standards may help explain why it seemed okay to have forty students in the classrooms of our youth. Those who fell by the wayside are largely forgotten by those who succeeded, but we have to remember what really happened to most of those forty. The myth of a golden educational past allows many of us to ignore the reality of inadequate commitment that has crushed expectations—and rekindled racism—for more than three decades.

And myths of the present have emerged as well. Our urban schools are viewed as scenes of daily violence unlike anything we adults ever witnessed in our day. Every time I tell people I teach in New York City, particularly if I mention Harlem, they think I'm taking my life in my hands. Similarly, the current teaching staffs are seen as composed of complacent but frightened teachers, our children as simultaneously abandoned, lazy, and overly indulged. Schools are assumed to be practicing a lot of modern pedagogy resembling nothing you or I experienced in our growing up years.

In fact, schools in our urban centers remain havens from violence for most children, which may be why we are so sensitive to any breaches in the wall of safety, however small. Although of course violence in urban children's lives generally has increased, I have been in hundreds of schools since I came back to New York City and have never witnessed a serious incident. They do occur, and a few a year are more than too many, and even small acts of intimidation and harassment, which we take far more seriously today, do impact on our sense of safety and should be intolerable. But life-threatening violence is not part of the daily routine in the vast majority of schools, and fear of violence has always been a part of the urban educational scene. (My own children avoided school bathrooms twenty-five years ago to avoid "hassles.")

Teachers are mostly unfrightened and hard-working, even if

too often boring, bored, or burnt out. Children, far from being lazy, work more hours than children did in my youth—although often for more materialistic purposes than I'd wish. And school practices have barely changed at all from when most Americans were young. Teachers are still telling and students still assume that remembering what they've been told is the road to success. These facts are acknowledged in particular cases, but the myths retain their hold, which helps explain why parents generally see "their" children's school as "okay," much like they remember it, yet join the larger public when it comes to seeing "*the* schools" as dens of iniquity.

A false story produces false villains and false solutions. The suspects are hardly surprising: teachers' unions, TV, drugs, divorce, working mothers, "diversity" (read: too many African-Americans and Latinos), welfare, permissiveness, single motherhood, the sexual revolution, feminism, relativism, the absence of school prayer or corporal punishment, lack of patriotism. If we but had the courage to boot out the troublemakers and reinstate the old standards the task of creating good schools would be no big deal. In today's code words, the whole thing "went sour" in the sixties. The fact that the 1960s signaled a shift in terms of who was staying in school and who was expected to succeed in school gets buried beneath the backlash against long-haired kids and radical protest, moral hedonism, and other real and presumed sins of that long-past decade.

To compound the problem, corporate leaders have suggested for decades that the economic problems they have been experiencing were the direct result of this alleged precipitous decline in educational standards—as though it was illiteracy or low SAT scores on the assembly line and not corporate miscalculations that undid Detroit! "Downsizing," the use of temporary employees, and the wholesale elimination of secure and dignified union jobs have been lauded by economists as new approaches to making America competitive, while allegedly low standards in education have been blamed for our unemployment problems. Myths and practices played side by side without much attention to their contradictions.

Schools offer a convenient target for blame during anxious times. But what makes them such a *great* target is that they often willingly accept the attack in the hopes that the attention will lead to more resources. It's like the class bad boy, who keeps hoping that if he acts up he'll get the attention he needs. Unfortunately it works the same way for both schools and kids. You get more attention, but not usually the right kind.

Where the Misplaced Attention Has Gotten Us

If the late 1970s were an era of malign neglect for education, a period of slow withdrawal from all the 1960s activism, schools were rediscovered by policymakers in the 1980s, with a heavy dose of mythology. Reports and TV specials appeared one after another, aimed at scaring everyone silly with their messages of declining standards and dire economic and moral consequences.

State governments responded with a flurry of get-tough, top-down legislation: minimum competency tests for kids and teachers, higher teaching salaries, minimum grade requirements for sports participation, and a lot more testing. This "first wave" of reform wasn't all bad news, but had little impact on life in the public schools. By mid-decade, governors, private and corporate foundation heads, and state and federal education policy leaders claimed to have reached the limit on top-down mandates and moved on to something called structural reforms—known in the education business as "the second wave." The leadership of the major think tanks—the National Alliance of Business, the Carnegie Corporation, and the Education Commission of the States, for example—acknowledged that the problem was not restoring old standards but inventing new ones, along with top-down support for fundamental "bottom-up" changes. They argued for the need to involve teachers and parents and to avoid blame-placing, for shifting the focus to school-by-school reform and the systems that provided support for school people.

But the think-tankers' reform packages remained largely on paper—heard mostly by the same people who prepared the reports or who attended the conferences where they were discussed. These restructuring notions seemed self-evident at educational gatherings but were rarely translated into either the popular media or good practice. (What did change a surprising number of classrooms was another strand of reform that was happening "back at the ranch." English teachers, for example, with their concern for the improvement of writing, sparked a shift in writing instruction that has had a widespread impact from the grass roots up with minimal notice from the Big Reformers.) The earlier talk of declining standards and getting tough remained what most people heard. Wherever I traveled, blame-placing was still the favored strategy. I found a grudging reluctance to talk about the need for new experiments, along with lots of suspicion. Why aren't schools more like they were in my youth? was far more common than, Why aren't they more different? If educators created the mess why should we trust them to unmake it? Proposed changes were generally resisted by those needed to carry them out—bureaucrats and practitioners alike. Change in educational outcomes, it appeared, was not going to happen as fast as the leading think tanks and educational gurus had hoped.

Given this climate of resistance, two simpler "systemic" solutions took center stage in the early 1990s. If bottom-up wasn't working well, one group of reformers had ready a new set of top-down mandates to take its place. This newest major reform initiative rested on a very old idea: increase the power of professional experts at the state and federal levels to require reforms through the institution of a uniform national curriculum (or standards) backed by national high-stakes tests. The other solution, also available by legislative mandate, was to abandon public control altogether, local *or* federal, in favor of the magic of the marketplace and competition—school vouchers, privatization schemes of one sort or another. Either local control or public control (or both!) must go, today's impatient reformers argue, because they impede needed change. In much the same way as schools are accustomed to adopt then drop guaranteed-

or-your-money-back curriculum or pedagogical packages, in a decade we adopted and dropped one after another highly touted school reform strategy.

Why Not Privatize?

Privatization has emerged as not merely the latest fad but one of the most tenacious of the reform ideas and a powerful threat to public education. We need to deal with it since it has developed a life of its own and rests on its own set of false claims about the role of competition in school improvement.

The case for privatization—providing citizens with vouchers to pay private school tuition, creating new publicly funded private schools, or taking the existing school system and turning it over to private managers—can sound compelling. The argument goes like this: Surely school people will be more responsive to their clients' wishes if their salaries rest on continued support and a competitor is already down the street or might be there tomorrow; the arrogance and run-arounds of public bureaucracies and civil service appointees wouldn't be quite so well-protected; to discourage privatization because it will improve things only for some is no more sensible than refusing to build any public parks or housing until we can guarantee the same for all. The concern that privatization will favor those already more favored would carry some weight, its supporters contend, if the public system we have weren't already set up to do precisely that. And there is evidence of a reasonable sort that even when dealing with more or less the same population, private schools have done a better job than typical public schools, at least in our urban areas. The argument for privatizing schools has been made well by John Chubb and Terry Moe in *Politics, Markets, and America's Schools*. It sounds even stronger if private schools are counterpoised not to the lay-controlled neighborhood school of yore but to the centralized, federally monitored and standardized schools we're being promised for tomorrow—they would make "opting out" seem even more desirable for those able to do so.

Of course, I believe that the case against privatization is strongest when rooted in the distinctive and essential strength of public schools—their connection to democratic public life. But while the central argument against privatization is the same as the argument for public education made in Chapter 1, it's worth making some separate observations.

First of all, if accountability (for fiscal integrity, fairness, or academic outcomes) often seems lacking in public schools, our experience with private enterprise makes it hard to imagine anything likely to do worse in this realm. If you have trouble reading your latest board of education report, try the corporate report you get as a stockholder. The same holds true for scandals in public and private spheres. While it's interesting that we rarely feel outrage or the need to "do something" when frustrated by private rather than public agencies, the impact of mismanagement on the user is much the same in both cases. One may grumble about how hard it is to visit one's local public school or get a clear explanation for how each dollar was spent, but try calling your local private school with such requests! We actually hold private businesses to much lower standards on these counts than we do our public schools.

Second, there is no evidence when it comes to private schools that competition has improved their product. What's true is that competition affects which schools get the "best" students (and thus can charge more) and which get the leftovers. You know a "good" school by how many students it can reject. Nor is there evidence that the private schools that have gone under did less well for their students than the schools that succeeded. And in fact, innovation remains the exception not the hallmark of private education.

Third, while private schools can and often do foster high-order thinking skills and responsible citizenship (as my own did a half century ago), they're not required to do so "fairly." In fact, built into what makes them able to compete successfully is their sense of privilege, including the privilege of turning students away for not being "our type," "up to par," or "of high potential." This dismissive view

77

of fellow citizens is not directed only at those of a different race, class, or gender, but also at students who are having a rough time and for whom success is not coming easily. The higher the reputation of the school the more it prizes itself on such selectivity, "cutting off the weaker limbs to enable the tree to grow stronger," as a friend of mine once put it to explain why certain children were dropped at each successive grade level from her school. "It wouldn't be fair to *them,*" she insisted.

We have more evidence than ever that such tracking by class or academic abilities is not good for educational outcomes even in their narrowest sense. But more is at stake. At a moment in history in which our destiny never depended more on reaching out beyond our immediate circles, the private necessity to do so has never been less frequently experienced. The capacity to create private enclaves in which everything from education to security is handled outside the public domain is reminiscent of too many science fiction tales that were intended to scare us a mere decade or so ago. Private institutions, after all, are suited to responding to their particular paying clientele, rather than to any larger common good. Even the best of private schools cannot rise far above such norms. While they proclaim their intention to train tomorrow's leaders, they forget that in a democracy this is not best done in the absence of those to be "led."

Fourth, we need to remember that for some proponents of privatization the motive is not personal self-interest but the self-interest of ideological, ethnic, linguistic, or religious group separatism. Although the church/state struggle has been with us for a long time, it is strengthened today by the alliance between the Catholic school systems' traditional interest in public subsidies for parochial schools and a growing Christian fundamentalist interest in undermining "godless" public schools and subsidizing Christian education. Other, smaller religious and ideological sects lend important support to this alliance in particular areas of the country. Their interest in privatization is based not on the virtues of the marketplace but on the virtue of getting public money for private, separatist concerns.

What all forms of privatization hold in common is a pulling back from concern for our shared public fate. They reward us for arriving at solutions that ignore, compete with, or even injure our neighbor's child without having to think about the possible consequences. No questions asked. In making private decisions parents never have to explain themselves or look their neighbor in the eye. It's strictly personal, after all. Who can blame you for doing the best for your own? No harm meant. The cumulative effect of our "private choices," especially on those least able to exercise choice in powerful ways, is thus blurred over until it appears to be another law of nature—some have better luck than others. The notion of the rearing of the young as a communal task is lost, begins even to sound silly and sentimental.

In the end, of course, the marketplace undermines the rationale for public funding. If we assume always the primacy of our private interests over our public ones we're not far away from claiming an absence of responsibility for the next generation by anyone but those directly interested—parents. Why should all citizens be expected to finance what is thus only a matter of individual private gain? Why should the childless? The old? But what then happens when parents alone must subsidize the full cost of education? As the public subsidy dwindles, naturally some will suffer far more than others.

Holding fast to the democratic promise of public education requires something hard but simple: a steadfast belief in the process of democracy, warts and all. It requires rejecting both the dictatorship of the marketplace and the dictatorship of the expert.

The Battle Lines

The irony of the fact that so many citizens have given up hope for public education and allowed once marginal issues to dominate the debate, is that the public schools remain one of the relatively most accessible institutions to democratic influence. And in fact the fight against public education is taking place in democratic and public forums. Schools are, after all, close at hand, less obscure and mysterious than a debate about NAFTA or even health policy. School issues can be seen and touched (maybe it would be a good idea to require "school duty," like jury duty, as part of every citizen's responsibility).

Unfortunately, most of the heat of the public debate is coming from only one direction. Organized religious fundamentalists have targeted public schools as the venue for promoting a national agenda that runs directly counter to democratic values, that holds intellectual skepticism to be a modern secular demon and sees empathy as a means of getting the young to identify with the wicked rather than with their own (approved) kind. The religious right has aggressively led local campaigns against "relativism," "New Age ideas," sex education, feminism, and "un-Americanism" in textbooks, new programs, and new pedagogies. For their own schools (or home schooling) they want the least amount of interference and the biggest amount of financial support. For public schools they want the reverse since they view public institutions as socialistic and godless.

Such extremism is not the norm even among fundamentalist Christians, but extremist influence is widespread and well financed enough to find the weak spots in public support for democratic education and fan casual suspicions and fears that ordinary citizens may harbor. Extremist tactics have been effective in defeating reform measures highly touted by all the major educational establishments in several key states like Pennsylvania, Connecticut, and Maryland, and in some pilot reform districts like Littleton, Colorado, and have kept others from tackling such reforms for fear of a divisive battle. While most of their audiences join the religious right only on this or that particular issue, the situation reminds us that the central ideas behind democracy have always been better defended in practice than in debate. Openness to new, sometimes even distressing ideas and to the kind of independent thought that makes one reexamine one's favorite axioms is not easy even among more moderate citizens.

In fact, we need to remember that many specific fears raised on the religious right are shared even by those hostile to fundamentalism and sympathetic to school reform, and that there are religious fundamentalists who support progressive educational ideas. The Central Park East schools have their fair share of Seventh-Day Adventists, Jehovah's Witnesses, Black Muslims, and fundamentalist Christians, who embrace CPE precisely for its openness to their ideas and its fairness in dealing with their children.

In demonizing the Right, or the Left, we avoid seeing our overlapping fears and our overlapping hopes. There are plenty of liberal-minded citizens who are uncomfortable with Central Park East's stress on open intellectual inquiry and would have us leave young minds free of uncertainties and openness until "later on" when they are "more prepared to face complexity." First, some argue, "fill the vessel" with neutral information and easily remembered and uplifting stories. But such compromises will neither satisfy the Right nor prepare our children's minds well for "later."

The habits conducive to free inquiry don't just happen with age and maturity. They take root slowly. And uncertainties, multiple viewpoints, the use of independent judgment, and pleasure in imaginative play aren't luxuries to be grafted on to the mind-set of a mature scholar, suited only to the gifted few, or offered after school on a voluntary basis to the children of parents inclined this way. It's my contention that these are the required habits of a sound citizenry, habits that take time and practice. But if skepticism and empathy run counter to the core of some religious values, ignoring the clash won't resolve it. These questions are the stuff of a good democratic debate for the minds and hearts of Americans. Defending secularism is not a problem only in the Middle East. The idea that a religious people can favor secularism has gotten lost in the United States, not just in Iran, even if the results are very different.

Many issues cut across secular and religious lines. Liberals too worry about what their children read. Staunch "lefties" occasionally berate us at CPE for not removing books with the "wrong" beliefs, and they're not always satisfied with our solution: write an attack and we'll post it or even include it in the back of the book. There are tough decisions to be made regarding the age-appropriateness of materials. It's not only the Right that's queasy about early sexual activity, or even early explicit talk about it. There are progressives like me who are not in favor of sex for the young, even *with* condoms. There are liberals who feel as passionately as conservatives when schools insensitively expose children to threatening issues. And all parents are angry when their children's schools demean their family's values or their community's competence.

The debate over educational reforms is not divorced from such timeless and mundane concerns. National figures and forums can stimulate discussion, provide information, give the debate broader language and scope without unhinging it from its roots. This is a debate about how best to raise our children—surely within our capacities. We need to enter the debate as fellow citizens. Teachers, parents, and students are among the experts that should be called in to testify. Only a community-centered debate will restore the public's stake in *their* public schools.

Most of all, since democratic schools are impossible to implement without an aware and supportive public, their defense requires us to tell the truth in all kinds of unexpected ways. Even when it gets complicated. Telling our fellow citizens that they didn't get the education they deserved in a way that will not be misheard isn't easy. Schools did the job they were asked to do—but never before have they done what is needed today. It will help if we explore ways to talk about the past that don't rest on nostalgia but on unearthed primary sources—how children really wrote, what they really read, and why they left school in such droves. At CPE, some of our best conversations with families involve sharing with kids our own educational histories.

Telling the truth requires us also to reassert another easily documented fact: schools are not the cause of any competitive disadvantage the United States may or may not face. American productivity remains high and American workers relatively well educated. They work longer and harder than workers in other industrial nations, and with less job security. There are, furthermore, plenty of "over-educated" amongst the unemployed. We needn't be ashamed of our country or our schools. The reason to reform our schools is that we believe in fairness and democracy. We can no longer defend the discrepancies between the haves and have-nots, nor pay the price for the social unrest these discrepancies create. Ultimately, if we stick together we can do far better for everyone.

People committed to public life, which includes public schools, must confront cynicism head-on, not look for backdoor solutions. Our commitment must start by wiping the slate clean of all the lies we've told and been told. If we're looking for explanations as to why a once proud system has failed, we are likely to miss the explanations we need. If we believe that the school we once knew—with phonics workbooks, familiar Friday tests, desks facing front, and teachers doing most of the telling—has disappeared along with the old standards, it's hard to see why we'd be in the mood to buy new reforms.

However, if we believe schools and children are much the same as they were in our youth, we're more open to considering whether it's not about time for a change. Then we're not talking about vast reforms that have failed, but reforms we've mostly never yet tried for anyone but a small elite.

Being clear about history can help. The myths of both past and present have given enormous advantage to the enemies of universal public education and progressive ideas about reform. The opposition has a good story to tell, and we often seem to have none. We apologize, regret, stammer, and give in step by step. Only when we can confidently build our case on the basis of a clearer and truer story will we be prepared to take the offensive again.

February 12

Spent our advisory time organizing a cake sale for our spring trip. I hate cake sales. But I go along. We don't need to raise much money (or do much planning) because we're going to my place in Hillsdale, and the school pays for travel. The kids always give me a hard time about "Why can't we bring a Walkman?" or "You mean you don't even have a TV?" But they end up enjoying it. Above all they enjoy the sheer leisure and play. Running around the fields, dashing in and out, playing silly tag games, shopping, cooking, giggling before the fire, keeping me up very late at night, choosing a movie, bowling. Plus the required trip to the college campus. Visiting different college campuses each year has a cumulative impact. But it's the informal opportunity to be together in this unhurried and "alien" setting that I love most. They remind me of the weekends I spent in the country with my own children and their friends. Differences of class, gender, and race disappear for me in this setting as they never entirely do in the midst of New York City and school.

No one wants to leave at the end of the three days. For a moment we feel like family. Magical moment.

JOURNAL

November 18

Last month we [the staff] wasted hours trying to decide on an approach to school life if the threatened custodial strike was called. This month we're trying to decide what to do if the Board wins its revenge on the UFT [United Federation of Teachers]. The Board's demand that teachers attend school for two extra days of "staff development" is now in arbitration. At stake: whether in a break with established practice teachers will be required to come to school the day after Thanksgiving and the first Monday of the Christmas holiday! As we await the arbitrator's decision, rumors fly: if teachers don't show up they'll be docked two days' pay. Our issue: should we try to find a face-saving way to slip by this or make a point of refusing? Since the chancellor is not the bad guy in this story, why give him a hard time? Our high visibility (and extensive extra staff development) tempts us to take a visible stand. The degree of rage it raises in me is unreasonable. In a year in which the Board is unable to offer teachers anything (class sizes are larger, salaries frozen, and kids are coming to school more damaged than usual) our "employers" have decided to pick a phony fight. God help us.

JOURNAL

November 27

The arbitrator ruled 100 percent in the UFT's favor. No extra days. Sweet victory. But what a lot of wasted time.

JOURNAL

Dear students, parents and staff

I recently had a conversation that gave me a good deal to think about. Two students had gotten into one of those stupid quarrels. The origins were silly. But what became clear was that one of the kids was a "victim"—over and over he was the subject of teasing and other minor cruelties on the part of his classmates. Everyone knows about it, including us adults. We worry, feel bad, get angry and end up doing very little good.

I asked the second student about it and he agreed that the other student was indeed the target of a lot of peer cruelty, and also that the reasons were silly, petty and unkind. "Which side are you on?" I asked. "His side or his tormentors'?"

We were both startled by my question. He said he wasn't really on any side.

I didn't stop, because I was busy thinking about it myself. So I pushed. "If someone is being cruel to someone else, if someone is the victimizer and someone the victim, rapist and raper, abused and abuser—can you really be neutral?"

He paused. "No," he said. "I'm never with the abusers."

What we realized was that there were two questions here and they were getting mixed up together. (1) Whose side am I on? and (2) What am I prepared to do about it?

The second is tough. Sometimes people lay down their lives for "their side." Literature and history are full of stories of heroic people. Sometimes they give money, extra time, put in a word, and on occasion they walk away guiltily or sadly because they feel they just can't make a difference or have other priorities. I feel strongly about what's going on in Bosnia—but I don't do a lot about it. Everyday I read at least one story in the newspaper that makes me angry—and I sigh and put it away. I see lots of things I don't like being done to others—and I often pass by. But I still know "whose side I'm on."

Be on the Right Side

But what to do—that second question—never arises for people who don't decide the first. We can't make a difference about everything we care about. But we can decide—almost instinctively—

87

always to be on the side of the wounded rather than the wounders. Taking a stand is just the first step; maybe that's why we try to avoid it. It doesn't dictate what we'll do next, but it dictates a stance, a "viewpoint." It sets some limits. At the very least it means we haven't joined the "other side."

I still don't know what we can do to put a stop to daily wanton cruelty that gets tolerated here at CPESS towards our fellow students. But my pledge to you is that I'm always on the side of those who are being treated unfairly, even if I don't always know what I can do to help them. What more ought I do? How might I make a difference?

CPESS Newsletter

Dear students, parents and staff

Last week I made a big plea for "taking a stand," "choosing sides," etc. It has been pointed out to me that life isn't always that simple. And that is true.

In fact, part of the purpose of CPESS is to make that complexity obvious, to force us all to look at the tougher choices.

Yeah . . . I'll admit that I forgot about that when I wrote last week.

Sometimes the "right" isn't all on one side. Sometimes there are what we call "unintended consequences"—we meant well, but it turns out bad. Sometimes everyone wants the same ends, they disagree on means. For example, some people who carry guns also want peace. They "just" think they're more likely to get peace being well armed. That's the argument for a big defense budget. There are bad guys who want war; but mostly we argue over the best way to get peace—on our terms.

But, and here's the big "but," sometimes it isn't complicated at all. It's very clear—to you and to me—who is right and who is wrong. Who is being cruel and who isn't. Who is the bully and who is the bullied. Even the "bad guys" agree! It may make them feel better to pretend the victims are getting what they deserve. People used to pretend that women who got raped were "asking for it." Racists claim what they are doing is—in the end—in the best interests of their victims too.

But you and I know that sometimes we see something that leaves us in no doubt. If we walk away, if we pretend not to see, or neutrally observe from the sidelines, our reasons aren't because "it's complicated." There are reasons to walk away—because we're scared, because we don't know how to help or because we have other priorities. But that's not the same as being neutral or joining the oppressors.

It may seem like a small point. A subtle distinction. But I claim it's a big one and at the heart of being a moral person. After that it's a matter of how much courage we have and how many other burdens we are carrying. I still don't know, for example, what to do when I see kids being cruel to other kids. We can't afford to ignore this kind of stuff at CPESS. Ignoring it is the start of a bad habit.

What do you think? What should I do?

CPESS NEWSLETTER

5 Choice Can Save Public Education

Conservatives of many hues claim to have the answer to reinvigorating American education: choice. Does the fact that District 4 is a district of choice vindicate conservative claims? Was our experiment made possible only by certain institutional facts operating in District 4, certain policy decisions made by the larger system? If so, what are the implications?

It's an important argument. Choice is a solution, its conservative advocates argue, that doesn't require throwing money at schools. The marketplace, the power of competition, they predict, will cure what a "socialistic" system of schooling has produced—the miseducation of our young. This is not merely a battle of words. A number of localities and states have initiated systems of choice, some of which open all schools to parental choice, others play with ways to give money to private schools or create a network of special publicly chartered schools. Finally, some turn over public institutions altogether to private-for-profit firms. What they share is a frustration with public bureaucracies. Where they differ is in their attitude toward public institutions per se. Some choice advocates—on the political right—make no bones about it: private is good, public is bad; private equals enterprising, public equals stifling bureaucracy and destructive political influence. A growing number of others are coming to see choice as a means to reinvent public institutions, to prove that equity need not lead to standardization and mediocrity.

The original right-wing challenge to public education—public vouchers to support private schools—went down to a resounding defeat, culminating in a much ballyhooed California referendum in the fall of 1993. The public was not prepared to abandon public institutions or subsidize private ones. At least not yet, and not in the context of the extreme form in which the question has appeared in most state referenda.

While vouchers have suffered a defeat, the idea of choice has not died but changed in form. Quasi-public charters, now popular in many states, may take the idea of choice one step closer to vouchers than public school advocates like, or they may provide a way to explore reinvented public institutions. Charter approaches vary from state to state, but what they share is a contractual relationship between the public and a school, and a funding and regulatory system that at this stage leaves many issues of equity and access problematic. Court challenges will be interesting to follow. In some cases legislation permits for-profit charters, and in other cases—as Al Shanker, president of the American Federation of Teachers, has pointed out—charters provide a way for millions of dollars to be funneled into the home schooling movement. Charters can thus easily become a means of subsidizing private education for the few rather than a way of unfettering public schools from unnecessary bureaucracy, which is what the charter movement's backers claim as the primary virtue of charters. Which direction this movement takes depends at least in part on how we see choice to begin with, and on whether we can proactively harness it to public ends.

Progressive policymakers and legislators have on the whole allowed their concern with equity to lead them to reflexively attack choice as inherently elitist (naturally, choice doesn't tend to make friends among educational bureaucrats, either). This is, I believe, a grave mistake. The argument over choice, unlike the one about private school vouchers, offers progressives an opportunity. After all, it wasn't so long ago that progressive educators were enthusiastically supporting schools of choice, usually called alternative schools. These alternatives were always on the fringe, as though the vast majority of schools were doing just fine. We now have a chance to make such alternatives the mainstream, not just for avant-garde "misfits" or "nerds" or "those most at risk."

While choice has been advocated by enemies of public education, I believe that choice is in fact an essential tool for saving public education.

Of course such a claim may seem counterintuitive, even shocking, to many current defenders of public education. When I first entered teaching, and when my own children began their long trek through urban public schools, I too was an unreconstructed advocate of the strictly zoned neighborhood school. I knew all about choice as a favorite tactic of racists escaping desegregation. There were even moments when I wished we could legally outlaw any selective public or private institutions, although I could readily see the risks (not to mention the political impossibility) of doing so. That's no longer the case. My change of heart has personal overtones: Central Park East has pioneered choice. The schools I founded—and in fact all District 4's schools—are small, largely self-governing, and pedagogically innovative schools of choice. They are schools with a focus, with staffs brought together around common ideas, free to shape a whole set of school parameters in accord with those ideas, all within an enormous public school system.

It would have been impossible to create these successful experiments without choice. Choice was a necessary prerequisite—not an end in itself, but a tool for effecting change. It was a strategy Superintendent Alvarado used to challenge the tradition of zoned, factory-style, bureaucratically controlled schools that has long been synonymous with urban public schooling and to replace it with a different image of what "public" could mean. Starting in 1974, District 4 changed the way thirteen-thousand mostly poor Latino and African-American youngsters got educated without pulling the rug out from under either parents or professionals. Superintendent Alvarado sidestepped resistance by building a parallel system of choice while the zoned schools remained as they were. Over time, even the proponents of the zoned schools—including their principals—

found themselves in effect beneficiaries of smaller and more manageable schools of *their* own design. Every school had become a school of choice.

To begin with, Alvarado initiated a few model schools open to parental choice, locating them within existing buildings where space was available. He wanted schools that would look excitingly different, that would have a loyal, if small, following among families and strong professional leadership. Alvarado and Alternative Schools Director Sy Fliegel gave such schools extraordinary support in the form of greater flexibility with regard to staffing, use of resources, organization of time, forms of assessment, and on-site advice and counseling. If more money was not available, more freedom was. When people in the "regular" schools complained of favoritism, Alvarado and Fliegel assured them that they'd be favorites too if they had some new ideas they wanted to try. Some even accepted the challenge. More freedom meant that the differences between schools were being acknowledged, not papered over, thus it became hopeless to tell parents or teachers that their school assignments would be determined bureaucratically.

Where there had been twenty-two schools in twenty-two buildings in 1974, less than ten years later fifty-one schools occupied twenty buildings. (Two buildings were closed by the city during this period, but Alvarado managed to add space by housing two new small schools in a neighborhood high school.) Only then did the superintendent announce Stage Two: henceforth no junior high would serve a specific geographic area. All families of incoming seventh-graders would have to choose. The district provided sixth-grade parents with lots of information to assist them in their choice, although probably word-of-mouth was the decisive factor (as it is in private schools). Sixteen neighborhood elementary schools remained intact, with space reserved first for those living within the designated zone, but Alvarado announced that parents were now free to shop around if space existed. And while the focus was on junior highs, the district also supported the creation of twenty alternative elementary schools, eight of them bilingual. As a result, the neighborhood elementary schools became both smaller and in effect also schools of choice. Alvarado even enticed a formerly independent elementary school to enter the public sector, leaving intact its parental governing board.

A majority of the new schools remained fairly traditional, although more focused in terms of their strengths (such as music, science, or journalism) and more intimate and family-oriented due to their small size. Smaller size also meant that regardless of the school's formal structure, all the participants were generally informally involved in decisions about school life. Most of the schools were designed by small groups of teachers tired of compromising what they thought were their most promising ideas. As a result, there was a level of energy and esprit, a sense of co-ownership that made these schools stand out. Over time they developed differences in pedagogy, style of leadership, forms of governance, tone, and climate. Only a few schools, including the three Central Park East schools, used this opening to try radically different forms of teaching and learning, testing and assessment, school/family collaboration, and staff self-government.

In this one small district, considered only a decade earlier to be one of the worst in the city, there were by 1984 dozens of schools with favorable citywide reputations and stature, alongside dozens of others that were decidedly more humane, schools where kids found it hard to fall through the cracks and teachers were more enthusiastic about teaching. A few were mediocre or worse; one or two had serious problems. Some were closed or phased out. A few of the more exciting ones lost their elan over time. But the consensus from the streams of observers who have come to see, and those who have studied the data, is that the change has been real and lasting. What's equally important, however, is that the stage was set for introducing educational ideas to parents and teachers in a setting in which they were more directly involved in decision making. It was not a cost-free idea, but the added expense was small compared with many other heralded reform efforts: the administrative cost per year for every newly created school was less than the salary of one additional teacher.

In the best of all possible worlds, the next ten years would have been used to carry out Stage Three. The district would have studied what was and was not happening within these fifty-three small schools, examined more closely the issue of equity, tracked their graduates over time, studied the families' reasons for their choices, and looked for strategies to prod schools into taking on tougher challenges. The Central Board of Education would have worked out ways to legitimize these "wildcat" schools while encouraging other districts to follow a similar path. Under the leadership of Alvarado's successor, Carlos Medina, District 4 launched Stage Three. But it was not the best of all worlds, and the district found itself on the defensive for reasons that had nothing to do with the education of children in its schools. As a result, Medina's efforts to move ahead were thwarted, and new leadership hostile to choice was installed.

Today, in 1994, District 4's schools of choice are secure, with new sympathetic leadership within both the district and the Central Board. That the fifty-three schools survived repeated assaults both from within and without a system that not only never officially acknowledged their existence but often worked to thwart them is a tribute to the loyalty and ingenuity that choice and co-ownership together engender. The district has been hobbled by lack of state and federal grants targeted for precisely the kind of work it pioneered, partly because of earlier criticisms and "exposés," and partly because of its own lack of boldness in tackling the more difficult educational challenges. Still, several new schools have begun, including an interesting new high school—the Urban Peace Academy.

The district's achievements in conventional terms, while not as impressive in recent years as they were ten years ago, continue to surpass those of similar low-income districts. They've taken a small but critical idea a long way. What they remind us, as much in their successes as their failures, is that choice offers an opportunity but doesn't by itself make schools good. Competition hasn't driven the less successful schools out of business, and the number of such unpopular schools remains far too high. (As is the case in private education, by the way.)

Objections and Risks

While the District 4 story suggests that choice is fully compatible with public education and an efficient vehicle for setting in motion critical school reforms, the story risks getting lost among the strong negative feelings, even fears, that public school advocates have about choice.

Many people think it's too risky. While our schools, they point out, are seriously undereducating all our students, they are failing some more than others. Public school advocates worry that choice, even if occasionally beneficial, will become a vehicle for creating an elite set of public schools that will increase—not narrow—the gap between the haves and have-nots, and that it will ultimately be used to undermine public education itself. Schools of choice are seen as stalking horses for privatizing schemes; the first step on a long and slippery road. Since I believe the United States badly needs both a more equitable system and a strong and vigorous public one, these dangers—which are real—must be addressed. If they are not understood and guarded against, choice, like any other reform, will be co-opted to serve the most powerful at the expense of the least powerful. District 4 will prove the exception, not the rule.

Broadly stated, Americans have long supported two levels of schooling. Whether schools are public or private, the social class of the students has been and continues to be the single most significant factor in determining how a school works and the intellectual values it promotes. The higher the student body's economic status, the meatier the curriculum, the more open-ended the discussion, the less rote and rigid the pedagogy, the more respectful the tone, the more rigorous the expectation, the greater the staff autonomy. John Goodlad's vast body of investigative data on classroom life, Jeannie Oake's study on tracking, and Ted Sizer's reportage on American high schools are benchmark confirmations of a simple fact: the biggest difference between schools (as well as between programs within schools) is not their publicness or privateness but the social and economic status of the students who attend them. What we need are strategies for giving to everyone what the rich have always valued. The rich, after all, have had both good public schools and good private schools. The good public ones looked a lot like the good private ones. The bad ones have looked alike, too. The difference has mainly been a question of the clientele the schools were intended to serve. If we intend to use choice to undermine this historic duality, then the kind of choice plan that is adopted will be more important than many advocates of choice acknowledge.

Historically, it was not a concern for equity that led to the concept of the geographically zoned school. After all, until 1954, neighbors of color often had to travel considerable distances away from the nearest neighborhood school. (And race probably still plays a subtle role in zoning.) In small-town and rural communities egalitarian ideals may have been promoted by neighborhood schools—shopkeepers' children mingled with mill children, ranchers' kids went to school with those of cowboys and migrants. In urban communities in the North, however, the poor, the children of immigrants, and racial minorities were rarely schooled together with those from more favored circumstances. Even when they occupied the same buildings, internal tracking practices generally ensured that they remained in separate worlds.

A full account of the history of public schooling might help us understand why the concept of the single-zone school developed such a seeming inevitability, but it will not tell us if that was the only possible route public education could have taken—or could take in the future. As District 4's story suggests, the notion that one's address determines one's school placement is not necessary to the survival of public education. The zoned public school may have been a convenience, and in a time when schooling itself was a minor factor in the development of our youth, with minimal impact on employment opportunities, this happenstance of history may have had only trivial consequences. This is no longer the case today. The school a student attends has a great impact on that student's potential for development and advancement. Since zoned schools are no guarantee of equity in a system where property taxes fund public education, and where internal tracking exacerbates inequities even for those who attend the same school, we need to rethink its favored status.

In part, my response to those who would dismiss choice as elitist is personal. I am irritated by the fact that so many concerned policymakers who oppose choice because of its potential impact on equity are already exercising choice for their own children. They are generally among the millions of well-intentioned citizens who have chosen private schools, gotten their children into selective or specialized public schools, moved to more affluent communities where the schools are better, or taken whatever measures were needed to see that their children qualified for classes for the gifted. Despite their recognition that such choices are likely to have negative consequences, they cannot resist. Writ larger, however, such individual acts have already fatally damaged most of our neighborhood schools and made change of the sort advocated by policymakers in place of choice nearly impossible. The system we have today is— despite all the rhetoric—chock full of choices that are not going to go away. There is little chance that we will eliminate the right of parents to select private schools. There is little chance that parents with means to do so will not shop around for neighborhoods with schools they find congenial. There is little chance that more advantaged parents will not do their best to get their youngsters into existing public schools of choice on the basis of influence or merit. There is no chance that parents with the power to do so will not use their advantage to get the best programs, classes, and teachers for their children within whatever school they find themselves. That is what being a good parent is all about, doing the best you can do for your child.

The more serious the impact of schooling on young people's future options, and the more critics decry the quality of the existing schools, the more parents will use whatever private powers of choice they possess. What we must do is shape the concept of choice into a consciously equitable instrument for restructuring public education so that over time all parents can have the kinds of choices the favored few now have, but in ways that serve rather than undercut public goals.

There is a pressing need for fast reform if only to turn the tide back toward public support for our children's schooling. Otherwise it's a continuous downward spiral that gets increasingly hard to reverse. Choice, as Sy Fliegel reminds us in *Miracle in East Harlem*, is not a silver bullet, but it's an essential catalyst. It can fairly quickly stem the flight from public schools, as it is doing in several key localities nationwide, and set loose otherwise demoralized parents and teachers to invent better solutions together. No mean feat. Desperation has led not just middle-class whites, but key public school activists, including many in the African-American and Latino community, to give up on public schooling. In some cities in which children of color predominate, such as Hartford and Baltimore, private for-profit companies have been invited in to take over all or part of the public system. The alienation of people historically committed to public education is a graver threat than the opposition of the free-marketeers, and public school choice offers them a way of sticking with rather than abandoning public schooling. That's good news.

But my primary reason for advocating choice is not that it will prevent flight, critical as that is. Nor is my advocacy based on the naive belief that parents and teachers will mostly choose to create schools like CPE. The primary reason is that choice may offer the only way to create schools that can experiment with the radically new pedagogical practices being wisely recommended by educators these days. Only in such schools of choice can we demonstrate on a sufficiently large scale, and over a sufficiently long period of time, the advantages of these new practices. Such innovations take time, patience, and commitment. As District 4's story suggests, the most efficient strategy for rapid change is undercutting the natural layers of resistance, not trying to bludgeon people into then accepting change. When edicts for change come from above, practitioners on whatever level they operate can and will undermine innovations they consider foolish, unnecessary, unpopular, dangerous, or wicked. With the support of parents and students, they can outwait the reformers. In a school my children attended, an innovative principal outlawed textbooks and basal readers; with the support of parents, most teachers found ways around his edict while he blithely thought he had shown great leadership. Parents and teachers have spent their lives finding ways around school policies—often bravely and to my quiet admiration, sometimes foolishly and to my dismay, but in any case such resistance cannot be wished or mandated away.

If the powerful consensus among the experts that pedagogy must change is correct, top-down mandates have pretty much reached their limits. We can't force-feed changes as fundamental as those we're proposing, but we can maximize the opportunity for parents and teachers to learn about new possibilities in nonthreatening ways, and—since they want the best for their kids—offer them the chance to join forces with the reformers rather than fighting them off. There are many parents and teachers out there ready tomorrow to explore change (sometimes just because they are so desperate) if we let them loose to do "their thing" in a responsible and publicly accountable way. They will not only provide examples for others to learn from, they will also help us figure out how to put theory into practice on a larger scale. Choice can make long-term experimentation possible in our public schools. We might thus be able to accumulate wisdom rather than endlessly recycling fads.

Choice has other virtues that recommend it in any case. It creates bonds between parents, teachers, and students that are in themselves important for any kind of schooling to succeed. We work harder where our loyalties are tapped and where we believe we have some power, if only the power to make a move. Finally, it creates the conditions that reinforce a sense of membership in a community, a quality that parents, teachers, and youngsters are missing in most areas of their lives today. We don't have to pretend that the marketplace will produce good schools, or that putting down the other guy's product improves one's own, or that schools work best if their staffs and families have a common religious or ideological viewpoint.

But once we cherish the idiosyncratic ways that schools solve problems, we'll have to also acknowledge the idiosyncratic reasons parents and teachers and kids have for choosing the school they want to be members of.

Making Choice Effective

To make choice an effective force for change we need to provide incentives to districts to break up large schools and redesign them into many small schools easily accessible to families on the basis of choice. Small size is a major factor in improving schools and an absolutely essential one for the kind of pedagogical exploration we are talking about. Neither parents nor teachers can begin to talk together about what they want to do in schools where meetings take place in auditoriums and face-to-face conversation is a rarity. Where schools are large and anonymous choices are largely made on the basis of who attends the school (high scorers, people like me), not the kind of education offered. Maximum sizes might even be mandated—three hundred for elementary schools and four hundred for high schools.

We will also need money. If we claim that all children can develop the intellectual competence we once expected of only the top 10 percent, we are launching a revolution that cannot be completed on a lean-and-mean budget. A variety of federal, state, and local initiatives that stimulate districts to adopt one or another variation on the District 4 story are also necessary if the money is not to be frittered away on more of the same. Schools might be given more funds, not less as is often the case today, if they are smaller. It's not a longer school instructional day, but better use of the 9:00 to 3:00 day that's needed first—which means resources used to "retool" teaching, and then time for the staff to talk with each other and with parents. Finding ways to provide supervised activities for young people when school is not in session is another and equally critical priority, although at this time it should probably not be confused with instructional goals.

While no system of rules and regulations can ensure equity, public policy must address the critical ways in which choice might adversely affect the least advantaged. The opponents of choice aren't being silly when they express the fear that choice could further segregate schools, siphon off the better students and the more active, wealthier, or more resourceful parents. Methods to ensure equitable resource allocation among such self-governing schools must be developed, but this is necessary with or without choice—tracking and special programs within existing schools compete for funds now. We will need guidelines that promote social, ethnic, racial, and academic diversity. We need to be alert to particular local circumstances. Schools of choice will, of course, have to be monitored regarding health, safety, and fiscal integrity. An agreed-upon list of indicators—regarding attendance, graduation rates, achievement, and so forth—can be used to suggest when and if intervention is required. With every regulation we add we need to remember, however, the dangers of presuming to solve all inequities by regulation.

Choice is a necessary but not sufficient part of a far larger strategy. Creating smaller and more focused educational communities, enhancing the climate of trust between families and schools, developing workable models of self-governance, increasing the heterogeneity of a school's population, and using pedagogies that respond to diverse learning styles and student interests are all factors that current research suggests correlate with improved school outcomes. All of these are far easier to accomplish in small schools of choice, and it is possible that many of them can be accomplished only in such a setting. But choice itself will not produce a single one of them, except perhaps a temporarily greater sense of membership. It is a vehicle for allowing us to move ahead more efficiently, not a guarantee that we will do so.

The alternative to privatization is good public education, and choice is the catalyst that opens the door for the kind of dramatic restructuring that most agree is needed to produce a far better educated citizenry. Virtually all the major educational task forces, for example, agree that dramatic changes will require removing and stifling regulations that presently keep schools tied to outmoded practices, to doing things in lockstep. They agree that if we want change we'll have to put up with non-conformity and some messiness. We'll have to allow those most involved (teachers, administrators, parents) to exercise greater on-site power to put their collective wisdom into practice. Once we do all this, however, school X and school Y are going to start doing things differently.

We can't expect the marketplace, public or private, to stimulate this kind of reform. Private schools aren't very inspiring when it comes to innovation (nor are private nursing homes, for that matter). In general they are as convention-bound as their public counterparts. They mostly differ in an invidious way, much like their public school sisters. There's a hierarchy among them, based mostly on how choosy the institution can be about whom it accepts. The fact that the choosiest schools attract higher-status families and select only the most promising students ensures their success. They cannot serve as general models; their value and advantages depend on their scarcity. But if the marketplace is not a magical answer, neither, experience suggests, can we expect that forced change from the top down will work any better. What results from such bureaucratically mandated change is anger and sabotage on the part of the unwilling, unready parents and professionals as well as the manipulation of data by ambitious bureaucrats and timid administrators. The end result: a gradual return to the status quo.

We do not need to buy into the rhetoric that too often surrounds choice: about the rigors of the marketplace, the virtues of private schooling, and the inherent mediocrity of public places and public spaces. By using choice judiciously we can have the virtues of the marketplace without some of its vices, and we can have the virtues of the best private schools without undermining public education.

November 13

As I was leaving school this evening after family conference I passed two parents in the stairwell. I said something pleasant; they barely answered. They were muttering; their son was walking apart. Uh-oh, I thought. Trouble. I found the adviser. Derek is new, tenth grade. His parents are mad because his adviser—Howie—referred to Derek's bullying behavior but hadn't called them about it earlier. His father made clear he found both Derek and Howie at fault. (Howie thinks the father treated him as the more serious offender.) He left Howie with a demand for instant feedback on Derek's future behavior. (Derek was a silent observer.) Of course Howie is now even more reluctant to call the family if problems arise. It's a trap. But how to get out?

JOURNAL

February 7

Remember Derek? I haven't given up. His father and I meet. He's proving to me that he's the boss. And I'm trying to suggest a way in which we can both be. Pretty soon we need to work Derek into this picture! It's partly an issue of race, partly gender. Partly this man's particular issue. Partly mine. But it's also his way of caring for his son. Idea: place the requirement to keep in touch in his hands. (Why didn't we think of this before?)

JOURNAL

6 Small Schools

I love big cities. Big schools, I used to imagine, might be like big cities, with collections of inner communities living side by side in uneasy but productive tension.

But reality has taught me otherwise. In schools, big doesn't work no matter how one slices the data. Large schools neither nourish the spirit nor educate the mind; except for a small elite who run the place and claim (falsely) to know everyone, what big schools do is remind most of us that we don't count for a lot.

There are at least six reasons why small schools (together with a mechanism for choice) are essential today, reasons that take on more powerful meaning if we want to meet the goal of ensuring that all children can and shall learn to use their minds in ways once reserved for a small elite. Small school size is not only a good idea but an absolute prerequisite for qualitative change in deep-seated habits, not just in rhetoric. And it doesn't depend on new buildings, just using the ones we have differently.

School change of the depth and breadth required, change that breaks with the traditions of our own schooling, cannot be undertaken by a faculty that is not convinced and involved. Even when teachers are engaged, it's tough to change the habits of a lifetime, embedded as such habits are in the way we talk about schooling and the way our students and their families expect it to be delivered.

Such a task must be the work of the participants themselves in a climate of self-governance.

The kind of changes required by today's agenda can only be the work of thoughtful teachers. Either we acknowledge and create conditions based on this fact, conditions for teachers to work collectively and collaboratively and openly, or we create conditions that encourage resistance, secrecy, and sabotage. Teachers who believe in spelling tests every Friday or are "hooked on phonics" sneak them in, even when they're taboo. And so do those who want good books or fewer workbooks, regardless of school regulations. The braver and more conscientious cheat the most, but even the timid can't practice well what they don't believe in. This is obviously an argument for why teachers (like parents) need the opportunity to work in schools of their choice, but it is also an argument for why these schools must be small.

Even if we're talking only about individual classrooms, size is important. But if we're talking about the creation of a thoughtful school culture size becomes decisive—especially if we're trying to create a changed culture. Thoughtfulness is time-consuming. Collaboration is time-consuming. The time they both consume can't all be private time, late-at-night at-home time. To find time for thoughtful discussion we need to create schools in which consensus is easy to arrive at while argument is encouraged (even fostered) and focused on those issues of teaching and learning close to teacher and student experiences, rather than on procedural rules and processes, elections and nominating committees, building-wide disciplinary codes, detention policies, filling out forms and checklists, scheduling, etc. Only in a small school can deep ongoing discussion take place in ways that produce change and involve the entire faculty—and even there, it's tough to sustain. For teachers to start thinking through the task before them, collectively and collaboratively, schools must be so small that governance does not become the topic of discussion but issues of education do, so small that the faculty as a whole becomes the decision-making body on questions of teaching and learning.

We bragged for years that CPE schools didn't have a single permanent committee. We were a committee of the whole; the time we spent talking had immediate repercussions affecting the way we thought and felt about children, classroom life, our teaching practices. If an issue arose we could meet with almost no notice, and gather together in one room, around one table or one circle, and hear each other out. We didn't need complex governing structures, committees of committees, representatives of representatives, differentiations of staff, classes and subclasses.

And even though on the high school level we now do have one permanent committee (our Cabinet), anyone can join any of its meetings—even kids if they wish. (It would be nice if they did so more often.) A third of the faculty is in the Cabinet, which only occasionally takes a vote. Mostly we argue it out and find a solution that all can live with for the time being. We avoid deciding issues better decided elsewhere. And anyone can insist that decisions made by the Cabinet be reviewed at a schoolwide meeting.

This continuing dialogue, face to face, over and over, is a powerful educative force. It is our primary form of staff development. When people ask me how we "train" new teachers, I say that the school itself is an educator for the kids and staff, it's its own staff development project. And it is by this same token always accessible to the outside world as well as to our students; the school itself is a public deliberative body whose existence is a reminder of the power of reasoning, reflecting, assessing, revising, and planning. The habits of mind, our five essential questions, and the habits of work we encourage in our students are thus exemplified in the daily life of the staff. We too weigh evidence, explore alternative viewpoints, conjecture about other possibilities, make connections, and ask, So what? We too must meet deadlines and keep our word and communicate clearly. We're "demonstrating" the value of what we preach—daily.

The staff spends all year reviewing its fourteen graduation requirements, and each fall comes up with new versions of one or another of them. The experience of our alumni/ae, of external visitors, the work of our colleagues across the nation as well as our own daily practice, all lead to such revisions. At various steps along the way the latest drafts are circulated and debated by students and teachers. We added a new section on computer literacy after considerable debate about whether it should be part of all our requirements or a separate one. Recently we added an emphasis on experimental science and redrafted the math requirements to better reflect the latest National Council of Teachers of Math (NCTM) standards.

Similarly, issues of behavior, school management, and student/teacher relations occupy our attention. We spent a good deal of time—even an embarrassing amount of time—debating student "dress codes," mostly shall they or shan't they be allowed to wear hats. But even this issue was argued on terms that allowed students to join us. People brought in articles about the impact of clothes and raised issues about the importance (or not) of worrying about how others see us and whether our informality would make it harder for kids to shift to more formal ways of dressing in more formal workplaces. The opponents of dress codes eventually won, but supporters occasionally still submit interesting pieces of evidence for their side.

In a small school we can dare to experiment without feeling we are treating kids like guinea pigs. After all, what doesn't work isn't irreversible. We can reschedule one afternoon and put a new agenda into practice the next morning. We can undo them just as fast. Changes don't require Herculean coordination or time-consuming bureaucratic arranging. In short, smallness makes democracy feasible in schools, and without democracy we won't be able to create the kind of profound rethinking the times demand.

The second reason for small schools is that if the faculty are to be held responsible for their work not individually but collectively, they must have access to each other's work. Only in a small school can teachers know who talks well but doesn't teach well, and vice versa. They know who is late, who is unprepared, and who in quiet and yet unexpected ways comes through for their kids and colleagues, goes the extra mile. They also can begin the difficult task of being as critical of each other as they are accustomed to being of their students, respecting their colleagues enough to ask hard questions of each other. Teachers may, of course, try to use their new-found collegial feeling only to make each other feel good, not to do good. That's possible. Teaching is tough work, and we often long for a friendly word and bristle at criticism. But as we confront this problem we'll remember that children too find learning tough and are sensitive to our criticism, and we'll see that support and criticism are not mutually exclusive. A small school provides the possibility of being accountable for our collective work.

Third, above all small schools mean we can get to know a student's work, the way he or she thinks. If it's thinking that we're seeking, then it's thinking we must get to observe, and this requires seeing children over time. It means passing them in the hall before and after we have taught them, knowing their other teachers well, seeing them in different settings and guises and thus developing a broader repertoire of ways to approach them. This close knowledge helps us demand more of them; we can be tougher without being insensitive and humiliating. It also means we know their moods and styles—whom to touch in a comforting way and whom to offer distance and space in times of stress. It means that every adult in the school feels responsible for every kid and has insights that when shared can open up a seemingly intractable situation to new possibilities.

Knowing one's students matters, including—and perhaps especially—those who are hardest to know. If teachers didn't do this for my son in his 3,500-student school, it wasn't that they were less thoughtful or observant. But he was just one student out of 150 that each teacher taught each semester. They didn't chat with other teachers about him, and when I came in for my annual dutiful parent conference they weren't to blame for being able to provide me only a list of his attendance and his scores on assignments and tests. There are those kids who find the one adult they need to survive, and others who become generally known by one and all—the school leaders, the school genius, the star athletes, and the problem kids. But the vast majority are more like my academically able and likable son. In his senior year he had a hard time finding a teacher who knew him well enough to write a college reference letter for him that would sound authentic. At a school like CPESS, the shyest and least engaged student would not have suffered the fate that the average big school student takes for granted.

Of course, knowing students and their families well also means it wouldn't have taken three months for me to find out my son was playing hooky. In small schools everyone knows everyone's business. Irksome, but also critical to rearing the young, and particularly important in a society in which few other safety nets exist for families and children.

Fourth, small schools offer safety—plain, ordinary physical safety. Teachers know when students are likely to explode and can respond rapidly. They can even get the whole school together to quell a rumor or redirect anger. They also know who belongs and who doesn't. They offer what metal detectors and guards cannot: the safety and security of being where you are known well by people who care for you. And there is less theft, vandalism, and graffiti in settings where people know us by name. The district's Alternative School Division keeps data that shockingly demonstrates the differential rate of incidents for the "regular" big high schools versus the irregular small ones, most of which—unlike CPESS—were organized precisely for the most incorrigible and unsuccessful high school dropouts or potential dropouts. It may be shocking, but it's hardly surprising.

Fifth, in small schools the accountability we owe to parents and the public is a matter of access, not of complex governing bodies or monitoring arrangements. In small schools we know quickly which teachers are absent, and don't need to depend on time clocks. In a small school we know which kids are doing their work and which aren't, where work has suddenly taken a nose-dive. If supplies are misused or disappear, we know that quickly, too, and can find out why. The school's formal leadership can be held accountable because they don't have the excuse of isolation and distance. They know if kids are reading by reading with them. They know about their staff's teaching not by scanning thick computer run-offs with complex tables, but by observing in classrooms and engaging in direct conversation. And they get to know the parents: in a school of three thousand no principal could ever shake the hand of every parent during the student's life in the school. Principals in huge schools survive by creating a climate in which most teachers and most parents don't expect to meet them, much less get to know them. The strategy is a matter of organizational necessity. The result is that administrators can be held accountable only for indirect indicators of performance because that's all they know—"standardized" stuff, easily manipulated and inauthentic.

Finally, only in small schools can we reasonably speak of immersing students in a culture that adults have played a significant role in shaping. In our large high schools, faculty life (insofar as it exists) takes its staff away from, not toward, its students. Students move about bereft of relationships with anyone but their exact age and grade peers. Adult and student cultures rarely interconnect, much less overlap. There is no thick, complex and powerful counterculture to balance the one that has been developed for adolescents only, no counterforce representing serious adult ideas and concerns to which these novices might now and then apprentice themselves. In part, after all, we teachers are trying to convert our children to a set of adult intellectual standards and appreciations— our love affair with literature and history, science and math, logic and reason, accuracy and precision, as well as our commitment to justice and fairness in the larger world. This in turn requires joint membership in an attractive community representing such values as well as a myriad of interactions across generations. Small schools produce innumerable natural opportunities for both. And they create numerous kinds of apprenticeships, not only between students and teachers, but between younger and older students at different stages and phases of expertise. They offer a chance, not a guarantee, that children will glimpse possibilities that make them want to be grown-ups.

We cannot convince kids that we cherish them in settings in which we cannot stop to mourn or to celebrate. In our big-city high schools, numbness becomes our salvation, as it does for our children, and in the process we become passion- and *com*passion-impaired.

We need schools small enough so that we can attend each other's funerals as well as confirmations, notice birthdays and weddings as well as haircuts or a new suit. We need schools small enough so that we don't groan and turn away at the thought of trying to do what professional jargon calls "articulation," but instead eagerly and easily exchange anecdotes and ideas about how to help each other and our children as they pass on from one grade or class to another.

Schooling is part of child rearing. It's the place society formally expresses itself to young people on what matters. We forgot that when we built our schools to be huge factories. Even factories know that workers need teams, gangs, a set of stable colleagues. Even factories don't change supervisors every forty-five minutes, not to mention work crews and job tasks. The army knows that the toughest work gets done well if the members of the squad have loyalty to each other, stick together over time, know each other well. Human solidarity is both an end in itself and a means to other worthy ends.

People sometimes criticized us at CPE for our devotion to smallness, saying it might lead to over-coddled, dependent kids who couldn't cope with the big bad cold world. We said they were wrong. Now the evidence is in. On a national scale our 90 percent college attendance rate is 50 percent *above* the norm, although predictions based on the demographics of our student body in terms of race, class, or family circumstance would have put it below. Strong relationships between adults and the young are good for kids. They're more important than all the so-called extras big schools can offer. That shouldn't be a surprise.

Small schools are not more expensive. We get the same per-student budget, dollar for dollar—minus the extras for dropout-prevention and drug-prevention programs that we don't qualify for! If we count the cost per graduate, we're amazingly cheap compared to many of our large sister schools. There are more than twenty large high schools in New York City (including all but two of the zoned high schools in the Bronx) in which only about one out of four students who enter ninth grade graduates. There are a half-dozen in which it's more like one in ten. Consider the cost per graduate in such schools, which is a legitimate question given that a diploma from high school is a minimal survival tool today. No method of building autos, no matter how "efficient" would be deemed economical if three out of four cars that came off the line didn't run.

Smallness, to be effective, must be accompanied by at least one other element, this one so intimately connected that I've been taking it for granted: sufficient autonomy to use one's smallness to advantage. It doesn't do us much good to know each other well if we can't use that knowledge. Nor do adults modeling good discourse serve much point if the discourse is only about the details, not ever about the big picture. Loyalties aren't engendered in schools that can't protect their own, that are controlled by rules that view adults and children as so many interchangeable parts.

In our large cities, at least, such autonomy is mostly nonexistent. Principals are urged to "share power" with their parents and staff as though they currently have power to share. They don't. Schools need to have power in order to share it. Of course, good principals covertly find ways to exercise power. But precisely because they're covert, these are powers that can't be shared publicly. We don't need to ask what power schools need. We should start with giving it all to them, including full power over budgets, and then ask what larger social good requires us to remove any of this power and lodge it in another place, and at what cost.

A small school must be a school—not a school-within-a-school (whatever that is) or a "mini-school" or a house or a family. It can be just one of many housed in a shared building, but a building does not equal a school. A school must be independent, with all that the word implies, with control over a sufficient number of parameters that count—budget, staffing, scheduling, and the specifics of curriculum and assessment, just to mention a few. And power indeed to put toilet paper in bathrooms. And mirrors, too.

Many parties have a right to a voice in decisions about public education—parents and the larger public being two obvious parties. But whatever their rights and responsibilities may be, we won't get the kinds of schools we need by focusing only on who has the right.

Unless the people who live in schools day in and day out, principally the kids and staff, are entrusted to use their intelligence on behalf of the task at hand, we'll not get change for the better. Anything else is inefficient, a waste of our precious time and resources.

A call for small schools turns out to be intimately connected with a call for choice. Once we create small, self-chosen, and largely autonomous communities, we'll have to face the right of youngsters and their families to choose between them, since no two will be alike. We'll have to confront competing claims on the limits of such choice, so that we meet our societal obligation to equity and diversity. We must acknowledge that where no competing claims are greater the people who join together to create a community should be volunteers not captives.

Small schools are thus helpful in preventing choice from becoming divisive and expensive, because parents can choose among many small schools located nearby. They can get to know such schools through direct observations as well as by word of mouth, not just by statistical indicators.

And small schools open the possibility, just the possibility, that we can replace our big high schools with something quite different. We can redesign what are, after all, merely brick and mortar buildings into campuses composed not only of many different schools, but of schools for children of different ages—and, if we are imaginative enough, other kinds of institutions that would live nicely side-by-side with the young. We could surround our children with true living communities in which old and young pass each other daily and are not violated into age/grade ghettos. The very existence of five-year-olds alongside teenagers at the CPE schools has had a startling impact. "Oops, watch your language. Don't you see the little kids!" I can just imagine the impact on teenagers of eating in cafeterias with adults, or passing by offices or artists' studios or labs where adults are at work. What would it be like if school buildings housed programs that their families were also attending? The small high schools now located on college campuses in New York City report a very different set of behavioral norms. College students, who often include other adults, rarely have verbal or physical confrontations with their peers, which makes such behavior naturally inappropriate, childish, in a way that adult-imposed expectations can't.

Long before we have figured out how to redesign classrooms, use computers and other advanced technologies, or do any of the other overwhelming innovations being daily touted, we can do away with one foolish mistake and proclaim that the day has come when every child is entitled to be in a school small enough that he or she can be known by name to every faculty member in the school and well known by at least a few of them, a school so small that family can easily come in and see the responsible adults and the responsible adults can easily and quickly see each other. What size is that exactly? It can't be *too* small, but surely it can't be larger than a few hundred! If that strikes us as shocking, we might for a moment look at the size of the average elite independent private school and wonder why we haven't learned this lesson until now.

On the question of size, there are no difficult trade-offs of the sort which so often accompany worthy experiments. I'm told— I *know*—that smallness means we can't offer as many different courses. But the average high school student in many large cities never makes it to the grades in which such choices become available. Furthermore, in a system of small schools in close proximity to each other nothing prevents a group of schools from freely choosing to collaborate in offering specialized courses. Or joining together to create a stronger athletic team or choir. Or using other community resources.

The one trade-off that sometimes may worry us is in its way also a blessing. Small schools are more vulnerable. Their very intimacy means personal relations can sometimes interfere with professional life. They need to guard against this, reminding themselves (as they remind their students), that you don't have to like all the people you work with. It can be tricky. Factionalism has even killed some small fledgling schools. (Then again, some schools need to be restarted; the demise of a school can also be a blessing.) And loyalties and personal affections can carry schools over rough spots. One year at CPE we invented a coteaching setting to help a teacher whose husband had died tragically, a solution that was not entirely within the rules but saved the day. The parents at the Bronx New School survived a successful attack on their school by a hostile district administration, and restored it to its original concept long after most people thought it was brain-dead. They succeeded because they were a tight community.

Small autonomous schools are, when all is said and done, a way to reestablish for us all, adults and children, the experience of community, of conversation, of the stuff of public as well as academic life. They expose us, young and old, to the workings of our political arrangements as we see how the politics of school life, the decisions made by kids and teachers, actually happen and how we can affect them.

Schools, big or small, can't create local economies, provide people with decent shelter, or stop the drug dealers, but smallness combined with self-governance can help educate the young to better cope with the present and find solutions for the future.

By engaging teachers, small schools stand a chance to engage their students, too. As we become capable of being strong, powerful, lifelong learners and citizens of our schools, so too will our students stand a better chance of being lifelong learners and citizens of a free society. Few young people imagine that adults have intense discussions around ideas, that what they are studying is influenced by what their teachers read and debate: arguing over the impact of voluntary versus forced migrations, what constitutes "our" canon, hearing each other out on words like "Eurocentric" and "Afrocentric," and considering how the concepts we introduce help or hinder our capacity to imagine "the other." Such discussions surprise visitors to our school, but above all they influence our students for whom these matters would otherwise be "academic."

It's exhausting work, at best. Still we dare not rest until we can look about us and say that there is not a *single* school to which we would not willingly—I don't say gladly, just willingly—send our own children. Small, self-governing public schools are the quickest and most efficient route to such an end.

Dear parents, students and staff

Family/School Forum: March 15. This was my first time, and I learned a great deal by attending. It helped me to sort out my ideas about what we mean by Trust. Our students were very articulate about how they see the issues. One student was also clear that there are times and situations in which there simply is nothing parents can do that won't make kids angry. That goes for us as adults too. But we all agreed (I think) that what teachers, parents and young people need to know is that trust *can* be regained and how. (It's easier lost than gained, many said.) Some people suggested that maybe we should break that big word down a bit—it's not an all or nothing business.

For example, if someone who is teaching me to drive says they don't yet "trust" me to drive alone, I know it isn't an attack on my maturity or integrity—just their expert opinion of my driving skill! Sometimes that's all adults mean when they say they don't yet "trust" their kids to handle something. Sometimes, as another parent noted, it means that she and her son just don't agree or start from different premises. Sometimes it means one thinks someone else hasn't yet had the appropriate experience to make wise decisions. In turn young people often feel the same way—that adults don't have the appropriate experience to know whether something is okay, because adults live in a different world. But, in both cases, it is often *heard* as a reflection of a lack of faith in the other person's honesty or good intentions. So maybe it would help to use less loaded words.

Trust matters a lot to kids. They read a lot into that word. One student said that her mother's and father's high opinion and respect for her was of great value and she would do a lot not to lose it.

Maybe mutual respect is what we're all looking for—which means feeling sure the other person acknowledges us, sees us for who we are—as their equal in value and importance. When there's enough respect, perhaps we're able to give up tight control over our youngsters, and give them more space to make their own decisions, including their own mistakes. What strikes me forcefully is how much adults and kids long for the same things.

I hope more of you will come next time. Parents, grandparents, kids—you can come by yourselves (with or without the rest of the family).

CPESS NEWSLETTER

7 Respect

When I began teaching part-time in the early 1960s, the hours and the vacations were important to me as a mother, and I thought elementary school teaching—the traditional woman's job—would be easy. Easy it wasn't, but paradoxically the difficulties I encountered so captured my imagination that I poured into this no longer transitory occupation all my varied interests and passions.

I found that teaching allowed for endless variety. The days were never the same. Each moment was full of idiosyncrasies, often thought-provoking, funny, or deeply moving. My job gave me autonomy as long as neither I nor my students annoyed others or tried to interfere with the way the rest of the school was organized. It was fun and stimulating in the same unexpected way motherhood had turned out to be.

Teaching called for every kind and form of knowledge. Nothing that might possibly fascinate me was irrelevant to my new professional calling. Greek gods, the properties of sand and sea, the motions of the earth, the legs of an insect, the nature and oddities of language, the stuff of myths and dreams—everything fit in somewhere. I took piano lessons again, armed with a new rationale—if I was indeed terrible at learning to read music, what a glorious opportunity to explore how many kids must feel about learning to read words. And finally, teaching was useful. Here was a place where I could make a difference in the lives of others!

I also liked the world of school, at least most of the time. I liked the noise of comings and goings, routines and rituals, unexpected crises, the parents with concerns much like my own, even some of the internal struggles, and of course the humor. Although I occasionally dreamed of teaching in a one-room schoolhouse in splendid isolation, I knew that such a world would not be as interesting to me.

It was in the hurly-burly complexity of trying to make ordinary schools work that I felt particularly challenged. These schools were, to children at least, the real world. It was within these buildings that the children struggled to make sense of friendships, power relations, and subject matter, and tried to square their new understandings with what they knew of the outside world. Although the world of school was artificial and the values within it strangely at odds with the children's family and community life, it still had its regularities and it was, as all institutions are, connected to the customs of the outer world. Sorting out the connections held value for me. I was startled into questioning assumptions that I had formerly accepted. I'd always been good at standardized tests, but only in reexamining them through the eyes of a six-year-old struggling to find the right answer did I understand how (and why) I had intuitively known which to select. As one quick with words, I reexamined the meaning of "quick" and the value placed on it.

The ways schools were organized (the homogeneous tracks, the division of students by age), their scale of virtues (where the worst sins involved talking out of turn or not standing properly in line, while generosity was barely noticed), the labels "academic" and "nonacademic" all offered glimpses into social history. Why, for example, was putting together a student newspaper nonacademic, whereas lessons in handwriting or filling in multiple-choice workbooks were academic? It was as though sheer authenticity lowered the value of the work. How could I explain the great triumph of the Little Rock school integration fight to young children attending an all-black, ostensibly unsegregated Chicago public school? Entering a foreign domain and seeing it both through the ideas of a stranger to public school life and through the eyes of five-year-olds created powerful dissonances. Conventional wisdom and common sense no longer seemed so wise or commonsensical.

What was for many teachers the source of discouragement and cynicism had precisely the opposite initial effect on me. It probably helped that I was neither very young nor inexperienced in life when I began teaching; therefore it never occurred to me that I needed to ask permission to do what I thought sensible. I probably suffered a bit from arrogance, and since I didn't want to settle for the kind of solutions that my colleagues accepted, I learned less from them than I could have; I unnecessarily avoided learning many tricks of the trade that later seemed so helpful and instead spent precious energy reinventing the wheel. These attitudes were thus sometimes hindrances, but they also helped me to see each experience, even the worst, as interesting.

I was also lucky that my first two principals were tolerant and that both the schools and the neighborhoods I lived in had a hand-ful of other teachers thinking along somewhat similar lines. And this was somewhat before the introduction of so much "teacher-proof" curriculum—learning systems and programs that turned teachers into managers rather than initiators. We were expected to be involved in developing curriculum, not just executing it. But we did so in considerable isolation from each other and we assumed that precollegiate teachers, unlike the faculties of universities, had no right to expect schools to be intellectually stimulating. What we were expected to get in return for our professional efforts was not intellectual stimulation but the satisfaction of our presumed dedi-cation to our students. As Seymour Sarason aptly puts it, "One of the unverbalized assumptions undergirding the organization and thrust of our schools is that the conditions that make schools inter-esting places for children can be created and sustained by teachers for whom these conditions exist only minimally, at best." We found our intellectual stimulation in private, behind closed doors. We never thought of defending it as our obligation as teachers much less as our right as human beings. Well, almost never.

It was precisely the privacy of the enterprise that I found most difficult. Although I cherished that closed classroom door for the autonomy it offered, as well as for the coziness it created for me and my students, I acutely missed adult colleagues. Few in the wider world I lived in willingly listened for long to all my stories about school life, or wanted, as I did, to ponder its mysteries. I was acutely aware of my defects as a teacher, of all the things that weren't working, the miracles I was not accomplishing, the ways in which I failed children. I found it intriguing, however, not discouraging. (If I could have dressed them up as weighty research or policy questions, my efforts to interest others might have been more acceptable.)

My own educational background as a student had been a sheltered one—independent private schools and elite colleges. My entry as a teacher into the public schools was therefore a stunning shock, repeated again and again as I moved from Chicago to Philadelphia and then New York. I remember the first and most striking reaction I had to Chicago's South Side public schools—that they were (and probably still are) the most disrespectful environments, even for adults, that I had ever experienced. Today I might not notice as acutely as I did then (I too have been numbed a bit by experience), but at that time I had no prior experience of being treated with such little respect or common courtesy, even as a child. Since my own children started in the Chicago public schools at the same time that I began to teach, I got a double dose of disrespect. As parent and as teacher it was much the same.

I recently came upon a letter I wrote during my first year as a substitute teacher in Chicago. In it I tell at length about my feeling of personal humiliation at the way I was treated by a host of clerks, secretaries, and school board officials and my difficulty in knowing how to respond. I wanted to walk out indignantly, to make it clear that I refused to be associated with an institution that would treat anyone so badly. But simultaneously I felt feisty. "They're not going to get rid of me so easily," I wrote. That spirit of resistance has stayed with me.

There is a special smell, taste, and feel to many elementary schools of petty humiliations imposed to remind teachers and children of who's the boss. I remember that when I began subbing I was daily informed where to report for work by a central school board operator who addressed me coolly as "Deborah" in a tone that made it clear that this was not a familiarity that suggested friendship or informality. I realized to what lengths I went to avoid interactions with the school officials who controlled my salary and job status because these occasions so often ended in humiliating tears of frustrated, powerless rage.

On my first day in a New York City public school, as I was delivering my own children, I saw a principal scolding a class for crossing over a line painted down the middle of the corridor. Their teacher stood silent. I quickly backed out of sight. The principal's tone conveyed something I felt embarrassed to have witnessed. Not only were the children being put in their place, their teacher was being publicly reminded of hers also.

Although I had seen these kinds of things before, in my subbing days in particular, they took on a new dimension. If I was going to make teaching my career, not just a passing fancy, could I work this way?

In the systems in which I have worked we teachers did not know our employment status until the first day of school, and we could be dropped or transferred without notice at various times in the course of the year. We had no choice regarding where we would teach, what grade, or under whom. Teachers clocked in and out, were expected to eat lunch with the children or hurriedly out of paper bags in makeshift teacher lounges. We rarely had much say in ordering supplies; having enough pencils became a major concern requiring feats of ingenuity. We rarely had time or permission to make a simple personal phone call. Even going to the bathroom required diplomacy. Our best moments with our students might be interrupted by loudspeaker announcements or office messengers. Sometimes principals prohibited us from leaving the school grounds even during the lunch hour. Some of these practices were modified by the development of teacher unions, particularly when a strong chapter chair conveyed a new sense of job rights to her, or more likely his, members.

The accepted rules for adults in most schools I knew were painfully reminiscent of those imposed on children. No wonder, then, that we competed for the principal's favors much the way that children do for their teacher's. We were treated like rivalrous siblings and vied with each other for more favorable working conditions or special breaks for our students. Collaboration largely revolved around gossip about the principal's mood, as if we were children trying to read their teacher's disposition.

I noticed that my peers were mostly women and my bosses generally men. Because 80 percent of all elementary school principals are men and 90 percent of teachers are women, it's no wonder I sensed the "women and children over here" syndrome.

Some teachers easily adapted to this subordinate position. Others, I discovered, used varied strategies to avoid the humiliations inherent in the administrator/teacher relationship. Some teachers responded in kind by demeaning students. Some teachers isolated themselves from the rest of the school, creating in effect their own one-room schoolhouses. Some developed crushes on their principals, or turned them into positive mother or father figures. A few took sides with their students against all rules and authorities. Some, mostly men, treated teaching as a stepping-stone to more prestigious activities—union leadership or school administration. Most teachers had learned some way to distance themselves from the experience, so that they became invulnerable to its emotional impact, placing their creative energies elsewhere. And of course many quit.

Although these strategies had life-saving value, I saw that they were also profoundly damaging to teaching. The withdrawal of intellectual, moral, and emotional attention allowed teachers to survive but took away the very adult strengths they needed to be good teachers, wise adults, and carriers of professional status. I fought, in turn, the urge toward each, but I didn't feel contempt for those who succumbed because I myself was always tempted.

To counteract the feeling of disrespect I felt subject to within the culture of the school, I aggressively announced myself as an elementary school teacher whenever an occasion to do so arose in the outside world. To my somewhat bitter amusement I found my well-meaning friends rushing to my defense. They would quickly assure others that in fact I was a very special kind of teacher, or, later, that I was really a teacher trainer or a principal. They felt I would otherwise seem less significant than they wished me to be. And the embarrassing fact is that I was often a little grateful.

And so when I had the opportunity in 1974 to set up a new public school in East Harlem, I chose to consider how to create the optimum conditions for making teaching as interesting to others as it had been to me, and at the same time how to offer the collegially respectful setting that I had missed. I assumed that if I could do these two things I would be well on my way to creating a good school. This meant inventing a different kind of role for myself as school leader. I didn't use the word "principal," not only because I wasn't paid as one but also because it was a title that carried with it too many negative connotations. It had long since lost its original meaning—principal teacher. I didn't—and still probably don't—view myself as "principal." I generally still announce myself as teacher.

Of course the most popular image/model of a reformist principal is not of a great teacher bringing teacherly insights to bear on governance, but of the bold, iron-fisted, charismatic leader who brings change by force of personality. We see the latter in the media, often achieving dramatic successes in adverse circumstances—the Joe Clarks of *Lean On Me* movie fame.

These heroic principals, like their legendary teacher counterparts, are often admirable and perhaps preferable to the principal or teacher as buffoon that we also often see on TV. They are Western movie–style giants who travel alone, thrive in places others fear to tread, and stay for but a brief interlude. Under present circumstances they are bound to be folk heroes. We see our schools as lawless Western towns, in need of a tall man in the saddle.

But it's important to remember that even at best these heroes are usually charismatic bullies (it's not surprising that they're rarely women), and that they sometimes confuse "law and order" with a disrespect for any law besides themselves. They revel in their aloneness and we are generally aware of an aura of violence that they bring with them. The violence of the young is quelled by counter-violence. The problem is not merely that there aren't enough such "leaders" to go around, but that these are not images of adulthood that encourage youngsters or teachers to use their minds well, to work collaboratively, or to respect the views of others. Models of such machismo have an impact. Their latent political consequences for a democratic society are dangerous. They are a product of both despair and loss of direction, of democratic ideals adrift.

While these occasional folk heroes ride high, most schools have settled for another image: the calm, businesslike administrative leader of things rather than people. Given what most principals actually *do* now, at least in large cities, a background in teaching (sometimes more and sometimes less distinguished) is of little consequence for the job. Nor do teachers often care whether their principals were once good or bad at teaching; the good administrator and manager seems an appropriate goal. These are indisputable facts, I believe. But sad ones.

All too often, what is demanded of principals, first of all, is keeping the ship afloat. The key word is "operator." Maintaining the daily imperatives—the doors open, the boiler operating, the payroll rolling, classes covered—consumes enormous energies. All steps to reform or restructure education risk the operational life of the school, which is often held together by the most makeshift arrangements. Under these circumstances it makes good sense to suggest that principals need not have ever been teachers. "People skills" may be valuable, but these can be generic.

But is there another vision, another alternative to either bringing in super-administrators with internships in "education appreciation" to run mindless mammoths or seeking a knight in shining armor to quell the unruly natives? Yes, there is an alternative. It's an old-fashioned one with roots in both the public and private sector. But it connects to a different idea of school.

The alternative presumes a school small enough so that the leadership of the school is not obliged to know his/her school by proxy, by indirect monitoring and accountability schemes. Such schools are led by people who have the respect of the governed— teachers, parents, and students. They are led by people who represent the values of the school itself, who lead by persuasion, not coercion, and who are accountable to those they serve. Their task involves raising issues, provoking reflection, inspiring people, holding up standards of work and competence. Their powers differ, their styles differ, but they are intensely involved in trying to understand the school as an educational institution and the issues it raises, which all fundamentally involve teaching/learning. The critical element of such leadership is the leader's awareness of the complexity of the task of teaching, a complexity that requires experiencing teaching itself, and not just briefly.

When I found myself, in 1974, the selected school leader, I wanted to deliberately reshape the role and ensure that whoever held it would retain the mind-set of a teacher, not an administrator. The entire school, I figured, would be my classroom. But it would also belong to all my colleagues. Children would stay in our new class—the whole school—for sometimes as long as seven years, not just one or two, and this would give us time to take a wider and deeper collective look at who they were and where they might be going. Thus for me it wouldn't be losing a classroom, but gaining an enlarged one. The constraints I had found so irksome as a teacher could clearly be loosened now, as we were free to manipulate some of them and eliminate others entirely. We could, to some degree, organize the schedule to suit teaching, order the materials we really needed, rearrange the budget in small but significant ways, utilize space more creatively, and relate to parents over the many years their children were in our school, thus providing a consistent and steady message about what we were trying to do.

The problem at first was to find a way of maintaining this teacher's mind-set while acknowledging a difference. How to create a collegial setting in which I was not quite just a colleague? Similarly, while I felt all the students were mine and the whole school my classroom, in another sense none of the students or classrooms were now mine. I had a hard time realizing that if the staff's job was to be not technicians carrying out my ideas but collaborators engaged in a shared challenge, then *my* dreams could not always take center stage. Furthermore, it took a sobering amount of time to imagine not my idealized self in each classroom, but the real people who came to work in the school.

I visited classes often, casually and informally. Sometimes I needlessly and impatiently inserted my views while visiting. Generally I tended to be respectful of the classroom teacher's setting and saved my critical remarks or "helpful suggestions" for later. Sometimes I joined as observer, another pair of eyes; sometimes to work with a group on an issue of interest to me or the teacher; sometimes at the teacher's request, to inform myself better about a particular child he or she was concerned about, or an area of the room or an aspect of the curriculum. Sometimes I took over the class so the teacher could take the day to be elsewhere or take a smaller group on a trip. Taking over a class was both humbling and gratifying. It helped me understand the particular problems described by a given teacher and how difficult it was to keep the whole thing afloat. It also helped me feel accountable and credible to the larger community and to parents—I "knew" from the inside all aspects of the school.

The balance between collaborator and supervisor was hard to maintain. I had many ideas, lots of pet theories, and years of waiting to try them out in a school of my own. I found that attempts to impose my methods were (not surprisingly) of minimal value to the staff and children. I fell back on what I had learned as a teacher. When I felt trusted I was more likely to seek advice, discuss my concerns, and, in time, arrive at the solutions that fit us best. It turned out that although trust took a long time to build—sometimes years—it was the most efficient form of staff development.

The same held true for relations with parents. While the closest ties are generally built between parents and individual teachers, the principal remains the representative of the school community as a whole. In a largely staff-governed school, the principal's job requires a special sense of balance so that parents don't feel shut out when things are not working well for them. Trusting the principal to represent more than the teacher's interpretation of schooling or of their child or family is critical. And this also takes years. It sometimes requires bringing in outside assistance to help school and family hear each other clearly. An angry parent confronting an angry teacher, where my sympathies lie heavily with my colleague, may need the presence of such an "outsider." But so do I, to be sure we really hear each other without my having to appear neutral. The use of such an external mediator needs to be seen as a sign not of defeat but of strength. We fell into it, of course, to help deal with crises, but then reached out for a regular relationship with individuals or organizations that both family and school could use comfortably when they needed a "third ear."

It turned out that the level of trust and the type of match required differed for each family and each teacher. What one person saw as a trivial matter was a question of principle to another. The appropriate social studies themes for the third grade, our method of teaching reading, the accepted standards of the language children could use, and the permissibility or not of chewing gum are examples of communal decisions that appeared major or minor to different people. To allow or not allow hats in school was a central debate for the first six years of the secondary school's life, a perennial joke—except that its outcome was crucial to a number of teachers, parents, and kids. Some thought wearing hats showed a lack of respect for the school and its members; for others any attempt to outlaw hats represented an attempt to infringe on young people's independence and honor. Both sides organized, rallied their troops to vote and were incensed at the notion that this was a trivial matter. It took six years to defuse the issue entirely; it's now remembered largely with humor. (The "no hats" side lost in a desultory vote after five years; by that time most no-hatters had been converted—although not me.)

For some parents, whether we taught phonics or not was a trivial matter, for others it seemed critical. Our decision to let the kids call us by our first names distressed some families. (This was a decision we made de facto, by deciding not to stop it, and which at first made me, the oldest person on the staff, uneasy.) We didn't change our policy, but we stopped, listened, and acknowledged the legitimacy of their concern: our acceptance of authority and responsibility. We also paid attention to the fact that we might well remember to take our cue from parents about how to address *them*. Finding ways to live with differences doesn't come easily if alternatives don't exist to conversion.

Because we value and respect each other, we have gone to considerable lengths to create consensus whenever possible. We find compromises or try to permit individual variations when they don't entail unacceptable educational risks. We have tried to limit the number of uncompromisable principles without limiting the vigor of our concern for such principles. Doing so is a lesson in democracy, we figure, and it's surprising how often we've been able to do it. Over time the knowledge that our colleagues cared enough not to outvote each other on matters that meant a lot to a minority— even to a minority of one—created a climate of openness and trust that was more powerful in policy-making than imposition by majority decision or administrative fiat. We began to really listen to each other. It became easier to pay close attention to other people's strongly held views because they were not seen as threats to anyone's autonomy. Although it always took prodding, as a result we also began to listen more carefully to parent criticisms of school practices and to external critics whom we invited in to take a look.

Of course trust presumes mutual respect. It means accepting the idea that a novice is not a lesser person, just a less experienced one. And this goes for the relationship between old and new teachers as well as between students and teachers. We must also acknowledge that we're not all alike in the way we express respect. Issues of race and ethnic background make respect all the more important, and all the more difficult. Cultural differences don't disappear because we are all people of good will, or have the children's interests at heart, although both these help. We need to get outside of our own definitions. In my family, mutual respect had a clear meaning, exemplified by a story my father loved to tell. Friday-night ritual required him to dine, he explained, with his parents. One Friday night, eager for an early release, he found himself agreeing to whatever proposition his father presented during the dinner-table conversation. "Yes, Poppa, you're right," he said over and over again, until his father finally exploded. "Such disrespect from my eldest son I never expected to hear!" Which is to say that I grew up in a family in which arguing was the ultimate sign of respect, and too-ready agreement the ultimate put-down. (It took me years to realize that not everyone was flattered by my challenges to debate.)

At CPE, small class sizes, knowing students and their families over several years, opportunities for casual conversation across age divides and around many topics, rules and regulations that largely assumed young and old have similar needs and rights (to use the bathroom and the telephone, to a place to talk privately, to good and bad days, to opportunities for telling "my side" of the story)—all these were necessary backdrops to mutual respect.

We tried to build into the school day ways to support the qualities we valued. Teachers, if they were to extend respect to their students, needed to be instrumental in decisions about curriculum and assessment. They had to be involved in hiring their colleagues and providing ongoing support to them. They were, in short, accountable for the work of the whole school. Which coworker would be next door or across the hall, which specialist a teacher would be dealing with, when lunch was served—the collective solutions to these daily problems laid the groundwork for interesting, reflective, and caring classrooms. Making this kind of sharing of power possible also meant that we had to make time for consultation and the exchange of information upon which to make sound decisions. It meant we needed more than the traditional once-a-month mandated after-school "principal's conference" (generally devoted to reading memos aloud to be sure that all directives have been "heard").

Reflectiveness required a different order of time. We learned that it takes months, even years, to see some ideas take shape. Above all, we recognized that caring for others is very hard to do if you don't see yourself as capable of being helpful to them. There is a terrible and seemingly pointless pain in powerless caring, and it erodes the capacity for affection. To hear a story and be faced with either ignoring it or being a martyr to everyone else's woes are the usual choices available. A school that is a community has other possibilities. When a former elementary school student called us years later, homeless and scared, between our dauntless social worker, Susan Bolitzer, our collective knowledge of the details of the student's life, and the organizational flexibility to mobilize resources and follow up on details, we not only found him a home, but located siblings lost to him in his infancy, whose whereabouts he had never known. At CPE we needed time and again to discover the ways to effectively care—to become better teachers. Part of it depended on having sufficient power.

We kept extensive notes and records of children's work, continuously experimenting with better ways to keep and use such information. We met to work out ways to sharpen our observational skill at understanding children's learning modes and preferences as individuals—what engaged them most deeply, how they responded to criticism best. In opening ourselves up to our colleagues and to outsiders, we had also to learn to deal with how we took criticism and to pay heed to our own ways of learning. We worked together to better organize curriculum as well as to increase our knowledge about the subjects that our students were studying. We exchanged articles and books we liked, and we attended all manner of courses and institutes that suited our interests and needs. Being seen as intellectually curious people, modeling what a mathematician, historian, or scientist does, are rock-bottom necessities if kids are to catch on to what we're about. Our desire to teach, after all, needs to be connected always to our enthusiasm and respect for what we are teaching about.

But aside from the time needed to collaborate on professional matters, the growth of trust involved individual and collective acts of mutual support both on and off the job—helping out when family tragedies struck, organizing the school so teachers could shift their schedules in times of crisis, chipping in when a colleague's purse was stolen or equipment vandalized, sharing the cost of babysitting so that all staff could attend weekend retreats or after-school meetings. Though camaraderie of this sort occasionally led to unprofessional collusion, our sense of collective ownership over the workplace mitigated this destructive side effect. Loyalty and solidarity are not always convenient, and occasionally they can be abused, but they are central to CPE's value system; they are the products of our increased trust and also the way in which trust is kept alive and healthy. (One reason why well-intended merit pay schemes can backfire is that they undermine solidarity.)

We even had to learn to accept the fact that at times some of us opted out, delegating power to make decisions to the rest of the group. Teaching is time-consuming, and our nonteaching lives often take precedence. After all, babies get born, loved ones die, marriages occur. And endless meetings can erode the desire to be a collaborator.

Good teachers are, I believe, called to teaching because they really like people—as unique, unpredictable, complex, never fully knowable, and endlessly varied. They're glad that the real world doesn't come with built-in multiple-choice boxes, precoded and ready to score. At CPE our driving and motivating idea was to make the world available to our students in ways that made it appear every bit as interesting to them as it seemed to us. "Uncertainties," my friend and colleague Alice Seletsky has written, "which are the source of so much concern and frustration, are the very elements that make teaching and learning such a lively business."

Over the twenty years we've been involved in creating the CPE schools, we've changed our minds about many things, scrapped some ideas and returned at times to others we once thought old-fashioned or passé. So many onetime certainties now seem problematic. But we haven't for a moment ceased insisting that schools should be respectful and interesting places for every one of us—children, teachers, and even principals.

What kept me going nearly thirty years ago when I accidentally got into this business is what still keeps me at it. Schools are the conscious embodiment of the way we want our next generation to understand their world and their place in it. It calls upon our most critical faculties to sort out what that message ought to be and how the teachers who represent the public in this enterprise can embody such ideals. If mutual respect is the bedrock condition necessary for a healthy democracy, then it must be the foundation of schooling. Making it so is an awesome and endlessly fascinating task. And fortunately it is also largely a joyous one.

November 1

Friday, 6 P.M.—in the country. I've been thinking about the argument we had at the staff Humanities meeting. Madeline began by showing us a series of drafts of an essay that a student worked on with her. To what extent had the student made changes just to please? How could one tell if the student learned from it? How did she decide what to edit? Was the edited version always better? What standards was the student basing his judgments on? But . . . it shifted into a larger "ideological" debate about teaching and learning, what kids don't know how to do and—implicitly?—who's at fault. I didn't help matters. I got off into my distaste for the kinds of reports we encourage (or at least don't discourage), as though writing dull, pointless lists about a country, people, topic (generally plagiarized from encyclopedias) is a "developmental stage" in children's writing. It was easy to make the shift because we're more comfortable talking in generalities rather than engaging in close observation of one child's work. We get restless. By the end everybody felt more inadequate than when we started! Hardly a helpful session, although lots of important things got said.

JOURNAL

November 15

I visited George's math class all morning. Lydia, age thirteen, was dispiritedly trying to complete her assignment: map your "dream house" on a sheet of 8″ × 11″ graph paper. I asked her what her scale was. Each little square is one foot. (Does she know the difference between feet and square feet?) That meant her bedrooms were $5' \times 7'$. We found a room that size. A large closet. Despair. The dilemma: her dream was a house big enough for her parents, two brothers, sister, herself and all their families-to-be. But no one could exceed 2,000 square feet. It's not possible, she said. I presented George with the problem; he recommended downsizing her dream. But then it's not my dream house, said Lydia. The constraints, George insisted, are important to get kids tackling the mathematical issues. He's right. Back to the drawing board. She showed me her first drawing, which was put together with four pieces of $8'' \times 11''$ graph pages. Her bedrooms were fine sizes. "But George said I had to put it all on one page," she lamented. Thus the cramped little rooms.

The project was all about scale, but alas, Lydia didn't get it. I showed her why the size of the paper didn't matter. Delight. The bedrooms instantly became $10' \times 14'$. To accommodate five families we decided on a dorm for all the children! However, I know by now that this breakthrough "aha" experience is only one more stage in a long journey before she "gets" the idea of scale. George was sure he had explained it. Wasn't she listening? I suspect he's a little annoyed at me for having caught one of his student's ignorance. He doesn't really accept that "telling" isn't teaching. Who does? We keep feeling sure that if we could but "tell it right . . ." (The noble fantasy that fuels every curriculum reform.)

JOURNAL

8 Reinventing Teaching

Teaching more than virtually any activity (aside from parenting, perhaps) depends on quick instinctive habits and behavior, and on deeply held ways of seeing and valuing. When a child asks if he can have another cookie, go to the bathroom, sharpen his pencil, move his seat, or stay indoors at recess, your answer carries with it a host of assumptions about what is and is not appropriate and why. Correcting a child's writing, calling on children who don't have their hands raised, complimenting a child on his or her clothing, deciding whether to intervene in a quarrel, pretending not to overhear a cruel tease—all carry messages of import, and all involve decisions that must be made instantaneously.

Every hour, teachers are confronted with literally hundreds of such decisions, unmonitored responses which cannot be mediated by cool calculation. Nothing is more unsettling in the presence of real-live students in real-live classrooms than an uncertain teacher searching for the right response! A doctor with questions about a patient's diagnosis can usually look up the answers in books or confer with a colleague before being required to commit to action. Lawyers and architects usually have a similar luxury. A teacher doesn't.

We think we know all about teaching; after all, by the time we become adults we've had prolonged contact with more teaching situations than those of any other occupation. Our instinctive responses to the kinds of tasks we confront daily were learned when we were children, not in our courses in Education 101. Parents, teachers, and children come into the schoolhouse knowing precisely what it is supposed to be like. If the expectations others have of us as well as those we have of ourselves, our habits of teaching and schooling, are so deeply rooted, is there any hope for the kind of school reform that would create very different institutions than those we've grown accustomed to? The answer will depend on how serious we are about the need to fundamentally change our expectations and on how long we're willing to stick with it.

For the kinds of changes necessary to transform American education, the work force of teachers must do three tough things more or less at once: change how they view learning itself, develop new habits of mind to go with their new cognitive understanding, and simultaneously develop new habits of work—habits that are collegial and public in nature, not solo and private as has been the custom in teaching. "Changing one's view" is what many schools of education think they've accomplished in their Foundations and Methods courses. But what kind of experience or mental shift is required before the difference between millions and billions is real to us? The kind of mental paradigm shift, the "aha" which is at the heart of learning, usually requires more than being told by an authority or shown a demonstration. And even those "aha" moments—like the ones many women had when we first began to talk with other women about our shared experiences in early 1970s consciousness-raising groups, for example—are hard to hold onto and often slip away in the press of daily habit. What is needed is not just new information about teaching/learning, not just more course work, but a new way of learning about learning.

And our schools must be the labs for learning about learning. Only if schools are run as places of reflective experimentation can we teach both children and their teachers simultaneously. (It's why John Dewey's famous University of Chicago elementary and secondary school was named the Lab School.) Schools must create a passion for learning not only among children but also among their teachers. In the words of Ginny Stile, a kindergarten teacher at

Reek Elementary School in Wisconsin, "It's my job to find the passion, to open eyes and weave a web of intrigue and surprise." Indeed, she notes, too many teachers are "passion-impaired." As Alice Seletsky (the friend and colleague I mentioned before) has said, "It's a little embarrassing to talk openly of love of teaching—this difficult, demanding, exhilarating, absorbing work. . . . But it's the best explanation I can offer . . . for the peculiar compulsion I have to continue doing it."

The motivator par excellence is our heart's desire, assuming we desire noticing the unexpected, finding an odd-ball but interesting fact that requires rethinking an old assumption, discovering a new author, getting pleasure from the way certain words sound together or hearing an idea expressed particularly aptly. Too many teachers who on their own time are immersed in such pursuits don't necessarily connect them to their professional lives. But even if we don't come into teaching with "desire," schools are good places for reigniting such pleasures, for experiencing daily the way a changed mind-set feels—especially when we're working out the unexpected dilemmas of a classroom that no longer fits the one in our head (or the one in the heads of our students and their families).

But the habits of schooling are deep, powerful, and hard to budge. No institution is more deeply entrenched in our habitual behavior than schools. For good reason. Aside from our many years of direct experience of being students, we have books, movies, TV shows, ads, games (remember Go to the Head of the Class?), and symbols that reinforce our view of what school is "spozed to be." Our everyday language and metaphors are built upon a kind of prototype of schoolhouse and classroom, with all its authoritarian, filling-up-the-empty-vessel, rote-learning assumptions. It's precisely such "routines" that schools have been expected to pass on to the young.

We laugh sometimes at CPE about how our students (and even our own children), many of whom have never attended any school but ours, still play "pretend school" in a traditional way—the desks are lined up, "the teacher" yells at "the children"! At the age of four,

141

my granddaughter Sarah loved playing school with me by acting like the mean old teacher I've strived not to be. She couldn't wait until she got to such a school.

Since we can't fill our schools with teachers who already have changed habits, what's the best we can do? If I could choose five qualities to look for in prospective teachers they would be (1) a self-conscious reflectiveness about how they themselves learn and (maybe even more) about how and when they *don't* learn; (2) a sympathy toward others, an appreciation of differences, an ability to imagine one's own "otherness"; (3) a willingness, better yet a taste, for working collaboratively; (4) a passion for having others share some of one's own interests; and then (5) a lot of perseverance, energy, and devotion to getting things right!

Asking for all five of these qualities is probably asking a lot, so we'll just have to create the kind of schools that will draw them out. That's what we mean when we say that schools, not separate teacher training institutions, must be the site of teacher training. That's why we fuss at schools of education for treating student teaching like an add-on, or expecting new teachers to rush out of school at 3:00 P.M. so they can get required credit at college courses rather than using the time to work with their colleagues. When we make our schools such sites we will have solved the problem of how to produce teachers for the future who aren't like the ones of the past.

We will change American education only insofar as we make all our schools educationally inspiring and intellectually challenging for teachers. It's not enough to worry about some decontextualized quality called "teacher morale" or "job satisfaction." Those words, like "self-esteem," are not stand-alones. What we need is a particular kind of job satisfaction that has as its anchor intellectual growth. The school itself must be intellectually stimulating, organized to make it hard for teachers to remain unthoughtful. Neither happy teachers nor happy students are our goal. High teacher (or student) morale needs to be viewed as a by-product of the wonderful ideas that are being examined under the most challenging circumstances. During our first year at CPESS we went around muttering under our breath a slogan we stole from Chaim Ginot: "Our job is not to make you kids happy, but to make you strong." That goes for teacher education, too.

Mindlessness as a habit may drive employers crazy, but it's a habit we have too often fostered in schools. The habit of falling back on excuses—"I had to," "That's the way it's supposed to be"—can only be rooted out by major surgery. It will be painful, and it won't all come out at once. Expecting teachers to take responsibility for the success of the whole school requires that they begin to accept responsibility for both their own and their colleagues' teaching— surely no overnight task. Schools in which teachers are in frequent conversation with each other about their work, have easy and nec- essary access to each other's classrooms, and have the time to de- velop common standards for student performance are the ones that will succeed in developing new habits in students *and* their teachers. Teachers need frequent and easy give and take with professionals from allied fields—that is one mark of a true professional. They need opportunities to speak and write publicly about their work, at- tend conferences, read professional journals, and discuss some- thing besides what they're going to do about Johnny on Monday. There must be some kind of combination of discomfiture and sup- port—focused always on what does and does not have an impact on children's learning.

Even at Central Park East after many years of such practice, many new teachers take years before they stop using "But I thought I had to" as an excuse for curriculum that they otherwise seem alien- ated from. Asked why they've ignored important social or scientific events rocking the world and their students' lives (the collapse of the Soviet Empire, the California earthquakes), they fall back on wor- rying about "covering" the curriculum as though at CPESS that mattered. "Coverage" remains a word we are all so accustomed to that it lingers long after we have formally abandoned the concept; we find it hard to leave a question or idea "unanswered" at the end of a class period, for fear our students will go home without having been told "the truth." Teaching as telling is hard to dislodge. Even when we're committed to supporting student-initiated inquiry, helping kids ask and answer their own puzzles, posing alternative possibilities, the desire for closure can overwhelm good sense. Suppose they reach the wrong conclusion, factually or morally? we fret, as though for the moment we believe the conclusion reached on Wednesday the 11th was the critical component of the lesson. Knowing the "five causes" of World War II becomes more important than investigating historical events, getting the Law of Motion stated right overwhelms the importance of seeing how such a law might be proved, and being against pollution comes to count more than seeing how complex and confusing preventing it might be in practice. We worry whenever we're not doing the talking, and because we're trying to change we worry when we are! Teachers who were good at the old style are often most troubled. They now spot the kids who are mentally goofing off; before, they took responsibility only for keeping the goof-offs entertained. Such formerly successful teachers miss being star performers day after day. And the ones who always had trouble with control must take time to discover how well organized and consistent they have to be if they are going to turn the initiative over to their students.

Clarity about what you're up to is now more important, but so are simple management issues. We hired Maja Apelman, an early childhood expert, to work with us when we started the secondary school to help teachers organize the room physically, to set out simple rituals of classroom life. Where should students put their work, their books, and their pencils if they were working in groups, not sitting in the same seat and row day after day? What should they do if their pencils break, if they run out of paper? What level of noise is appropriate? If everyone is not in the same place in the same textbook, turning in the same homework, how do teachers keep track? And how can you learn to do these all at once?

Lots of teachers come to this practice thinking that now they can relax and go with the flow, but in an odd way, in "freeing" the classroom from past traditions we've made teachers less free to do so. If all eyes are face-forward on the teacher, the teacher doesn't have to be well organized. Planning may be a good thing but you can "wing it" if all you're doing is talking. However, unless teachers are dispensing with their role entirely, being well prepared is paramount in the classrooms we hope for.

In the early years of CPE we invited a great teacher from London, Wendla Kernig, to work in a classroom at our school for a week while teachers took turns sitting in a loft observing. She spent the morning teaching and then in the afternoon took us through all the decisions she had made in the course of three hours of interactions with kids and showed us her list of necessary follow-ups in preparation for the next day. "I need red markers, a book on insects, some good samples of dialogue," and on and on. It was a never-forgotten demonstration of the kind of intellectual preparedness that goes into thoughtful teaching. Wendla Kernig brought together the traditional teacher's capacity for authoritative "telling," when it was called for, with appropriate opportunities for children to see for themselves when that was what was needed.

At CPE schools we see to it that teachers work with other professionals external to the school, visit other schools, have time to speak and write about their practice. The larger system provides the whole school with only two days of professional time off a year, so that just two teachers can each do something professional for one day apiece. We've found ways around that because it's contrary to good practice and furthermore lends itself to a misleading view of adulthood. Students need to know that grown-ups are also learners.

How to Get There from Here?

It is not possible to escape the pain of producing such changed practice by magically innoculating the next generation with a different set of habits, bypassing both current teachers and parents. It's the old pulling oneself up by the bootstraps problem. Every revolutionary political ideology comes up against this same conundrum, and historically most revolutionaries have thought they could resolve it only by totalitarian measures. Some (look at the varied schemes of the Soviet Union or Communist China) have tried removing children from their families, sowing suspicion between generations, forcing prescriptive ideological training from infancy on up, or creating a network of Big Brothers watching. They hope thus to breed a new generation that leaps over the weaknesses of the present misguided and corrupted one. The early Zionists had similar hopes for communal child-rearing on the kibbutz. (The kibbutz was a far more benign but not much more successful attempt to bypass the older generation, although there are aspects of that experiment worth learning from.)

Most school reform efforts are not so different in conception, if milder in action. So-called revolutionary school reform, for example, often rests on the creation of "teacher-proof" curricula, on testing and monitoring, penalties and threats. These strategies in schools will have no more luck than their political cousins. They share the same flawed assumptions about the relationship between means and ends, and thus they always miss the boat.

One cannot impose real change from above, at least not for long, nor isolate one generation from the next—not only because it's immoral or unpleasant, but because it doesn't work. And the price paid for trying to wipe out the past by fiat is enormous. It is illogical to imagine that we can produce thoughtful and critical thinkers by rote imposition or that we can build strong intellectual understanding by imposing massive change from above and pretending that it doesn't matter what the implementers of change think or feel.

We cannot pass on to a new generation that which we do not ourselves possess! That's the conundrum. The seemingly impossible paradox. As Michelle Fine puts it, "We can only work with the pictures we have in our head."

How might we approach such a riddle? Create those "lab schools" described earlier, where new pictures can emerge. Our schools must lead the way toward their own liberation. As Eugene V. Debs said in the context of another revolutionary dream, "I would not lead you to the promised land, because if I could lead you there, so others could lead you back."

Thirty years ago, teachers were force-marched to the promised land of "new math," and the results should be a reminder. Impatience for a rapid improvement in math education following Sputnik doomed the effort to failure, and today we are once again trying to introduce just such a math education. For all the humor with which we look back upon the brave effort of the 1960s to introduce a more sophisticated, hands-on math—with talk of set theory, and nonstandard measurement, and alternatives to the decimal system and ever so many other novelties—"new math" was essentially the same set of ideas that has reemerged in the new National Council of Teachers of Mathematics frameworks. In between we scrapped most of the new textbooks, taught kids some of it by the same old rote methods, and put back into our closets all the fancy hands-on rods, chips, and abacuses that we had thought might help them understand what numeracy was all about. Had we been more patient thirty years ago we'd be thirty years ahead of the game now. Had we accepted the idea that it would take a few decades to help bewildered and thus embarrassed parents and teachers deal with "new math"—not rushed them into it because it was "correct" and then abandoned it because they were too "stupid"—we'd have something to show for it now, and could introduce the next new math as a further step forward, not as though it were invented only yesterday.

The only route possible is to involve all parties to education in the process of reinventing schooling. It's our mind-set that needs changing, along with the institutional arrangements that either support or impede a new one. But you don't and shouldn't fool with people's mind-sets loosely. We're talking about changes that will affect not just teachers (although without them it's pointless) but also their constituents—parents and children. It is through collective co-ownership of new designs of schooling in an atmosphere that allows for reflective examination and reshaping based on experience that something new might emerge.

Time is critical here. Parents need to feel that they can continue to provide support to their children in "the old ways." No big deal if kids learn things through alternate methods. It might even be good practice for schools to show kids such alternatives, to help kids see them as legitimate; it would, in its way, be a lesson in multiple perspectives. Generational differences are in some ways a part of the multiculturalism we're interested in.

The habit of respect for old ways is important for the young, too. Teaching kids the history of change, so that they respect the old ideas as well as the new ones, isn't such a bad idea even in science and math. We know in science teaching, for example, how much damage is done by not stopping to acknowledge the way the world "seems" to the naive viewer—flat. The ideas we hold in our head don't get dislodged just because new ones come along with greater authority attached to them. Rather we tack the new ones onto our old ideas, often inappropriately unless we have help. The help needed depends on a teacher (official or otherwise) who brings the old to the surface rather than letting it hide unacknowledged. The discovery that light moves in straight lines is a "ho-hum" for kids until they have the opportunity to think about how else it might move, and what "move" means, and what they thought before the physics lesson began, not to mention what generations of other smart people once believed about light. Only then can they begin to accommodate these many conflicting theories.

Changing our "commonsense" ideas when in fact they are not completely accurate (sometimes they're completely *in*accurate) is not an overnight event or the result of a single lecture, demonstration, course, or even year of study. This is a very conservative idea of how ideas change, but also profoundly radical in its implications. If we want the next generation to be truly better educated on such matters, then they need a setting in which they are expected to "cover" a lot less so that such new habits of thought can take root— a setting in which they can practice, get feedback, and try again as new ideas gradually begin to make sense. Even one "aha" by itself is not enough, much less answering the question right at the end of the chapter.

Except for those few who had themselves been products of somewhat "progressive" schools in their own childhood, most teachers need to feel free to move back and forth, at their own pace, between the new habits they are trying out and the old ones they are theoretically abandoning. There will come a moment when the tension between old and new becomes a hindrance and the leap forward must be made, the paradigm shift completed.

We're at such a moment at CPESS. We knew from the start that we were heading toward a different system of graduation, one that no longer depended on a set number of course credits, and that this would affect how we viewed course grades. But in the meantime, since we didn't yet have the next step in place, we weren't ready to replace traditional grades completely (A's, B's, C's, or numerical grades). We temporized with Satisfactory and Incomplete. Then we added Distinguished, and put in plusses and minuses and an Unsatisfactory which was not the same as an Incomplete. Teachers produced different "scoring grids" to justify these varied separate categories (nearly ten in all). We worked at agreeing on a common set of criteria. But the more we worked at it the more complex our systems became and the less relevance the grade had to our parallel development of exhibitions, portfolios, and graduation committees. Now we simply have both, and the contradictions between them are showing up and confusing issues. We adapt. But uncomfortably. Sometime soon we'll need to tackle the conflict the systems represent, two different ways of "counting" what matters. But while the school's directors are free to nudge and question, hoping to move the timetable up a bit, the staff won't successfully tackle this until they're ready. It might even be that students or parents will be the best instigators of the next move.

As we've learned at Central Park East, changing our educational ways will be at least exhausting, at times frustrating. The only thing we keep telling our colleagues in other schools is that the path surely won't lead to burn-out because people only burn out when they're treated like appliances. This kind of teaching and schooling is never dehumanizing because it rests upon intense human interaction and involvement.

People's habits change only when they have strong reasons to want to change, and a conducive environment. For teachers this means that they need sufficient support from those they depend on—school boards, administrators, parents—to take some risky first steps. They need, furthermore, the luxury of being able to "waste" money on ideas that may turn out not to work, rather than feeling obliged to pretend that everything they do is successful. They need access to expertise without promising to follow expert advice. They need time. They need time in a daily, weekly, monthly sense—to reflect, examine, redo. They also need the other kind of time—the years it will take to see it through. These are the conditions that paradoxically apply whenever we're in a hurry to do something difficult: cure cancer, go to the moon, invent new technologies.

The greater the desire for change on the part of teachers, parents, and kids, the less it will cost. True converts are willing to work overtime, but their numbers will be small at first. We won't get large-scale school reform in America if we count only on such zealots. Money (translate: extra personnel, financial incentives, paid time, equipment) can compensate for zeal where the latter is in short supply. But we'd be foolish not to give the ardent reformers the room and space to work their hearts out as we build up credibility for more ambitious, and more expensive, national efforts.

My longtime school ally Ann Cook came back from visiting General Motors' new Saturn plant in Tennessee and was staggered by its innovative team approach. But, she noted, the average Saturn employee gets four weeks a year for staff development—each and every employee! In most of our nation's schools two or three days is generous. Resources are also needed to provide decent space. Our urban schools are overcrowded, and if we had the kinds of schools we've been describing they'd be twice as strained. At CPE we've sacrificed to create classes of less than twenty students and advisory loads of less than fifteen; that means 50 percent more room space is needed! We've created libraries and art studios that are open at all hours for individuals or groups to use. That means more space. Unlike most industries, we can't retool by closing down the factories while we build new ones and send all the workers back to school for retraining. We need to do everything at once. It's driving while changing the tires, not to mention the transmission system.

We based our work at CPE on simple principles familiar enough to those who work with young children, but less familiar to those who work with adolescents or adults.

For example, we knew that five-year-olds learn best when they feel relatively safe physically as well as psychically. (Little kids need to feel comfortable about going to the bathroom, for example. How about teenagers? How about teachers?) Feeling safe includes trusting at least some of those "in charge," not to mention being able to predict with some degree of accuracy how the place works. For young children we know it also means that parents need to see the school as safe so that they can reassure their children that "those people are okay, you can trust them to care for you." It turns out that this is also critical for the development of fifteen-year-olds. They too suffer if they come to school carrying warnings from their families. The appropriate rebellion of adolescence can't be carried out successfully in a setting in which the adults are seen as dangerous. Healthy "testing out" rests upon a basic trust that there are adults prepared to set limits. Is it so different at fifty? Don't we all need a workplace that is safe, predictable, and on our side? But just as safety is critical to learning, so too are opportunities to observe experts. Novices learn from others more expert than they. In kindergarten we don't group kids so that only those who are "good at" sand play can work together. And we don't expect children to learn songs that they haven't heard others sing before them. Telling about music doesn't get us far at the age of five, nor does telling about science work much better at fifteen.

A second principle: size and scale are critical. Even prisons and army units aren't as huge, impersonal, and anonymous as many schools are for children. And it's not just children who suffer from a depersonalization of work, it's adults, too. All but a few stars become lookers-on, admirers, or wallflowers, not active participants.

Our third principle is an old familiar one: you can't be an effective coach or expert if you are also judge and high executioner.

As my son explained to me one day when I was trying to convince him to ask his teacher to explain something to him, "Mom, you don't understand. The *last* person in the world I'd let know if I don't understand is my *teacher*." Too often schooling becomes a vast game in which teachers try to trick students into revealing their ignorance while students try to trick teachers into not noticing it. Getting a good grade, after all, is getting the teacher to think you know more than you do! Is it so different for teachers, whose only source of help and support is precisely the person who rates and rules them? The Coalition of Essential Schools metaphor "teacher as coach" is full of possibilities not only for the relationship between adults and children, but for all teaching/learning settings.

A fourth principle for an efficient learning environment is that we take advantage of the fact that we learn best when our natural drive to make sense of things is allowed to flourish. A seven-year-old who insists that $3+4=12$ is right (even though on closer examination it makes no sense even to him) because "the teacher told me so" is not being ornery, he just thinks it quite possible for $3+4$ to be 7 in real life and 12 in school. And he'll fight you tooth and nail if you try to show him that maybe he got his plus and times signs mixed up. He's grown accustomed to the idea that school math doesn't have to make sense. Under such circumstances it doesn't much matter whether the curriculum is about things of interest or not, in fact it may even help if it is clearly irrelevant (the temptation to try to make sense of it won't be so great). Only if we want to encourage "sense making" at school is it of value to build a curriculum around topics a student is either curious or knowledgeable about. Human beings by nature want the puzzle to fit together, but not all puzzles at all times. From the moment of birth until death this is our preeminent mode. We tackle first one thing and then another as our interests and competencies shift. Schools rarely capitalize on this once children pass the magic age of five. A nursery school teacher uses the room itself to create interest and curiosity. She carefully sets up the environment with interesting objects and apparatus so that it invites questions, and she spends her time moving about the room, prodding, inquiring, changing materials and tools so that curiosity is kept lively and current. She creates dissonances as well as harmonies; she creates confusion as well as serenity. Contradictions are accepted as natural, even necessary to the learning animal.

By the time students reach high school we have stripped the environment bare, and lessons are dry and "clear-cut"; confusion may reign but not for any useful purpose. No high school teacher (and surely not a college professor) worthy of his or her salt is allowed to admit that the actual physical setting of his/her classroom is a relevant part of the job! And our typical explanation for why we teach what we do is that it's required at the next grade level or, later, on a licensure exam. I once did a survey of second-graders on why they needed to learn to read. Almost to a child they never got beyond school-referential answers: to pass to third, fourth, fifth grade, to get into college, to read to your child so he can do well in school, and on and on. Try asking a random sample of adults why we teach calculus and you might get a similar range of answers. Teaching and learning becomes simplified, stripped down, focusing more and more on skill at taking tests where everything has one and only one answer. Nor do teachers view the courses they are required to take to get a license or upgrade their status much differently. Teachers' own interests are often irrelevant, at best sneaked into the high school schedule. We're more concerned with covering things than getting to the heart of a subject by immersing kids in the language and nature of that subject. What we now know about how best to learn a new language—by immersion—is no less true in any other domain.

Finally, human beings are by nature social, interactive learners. We observe how others do it and see if it works for us. We learn to drive and cook this way. And how to handle ideas. We check out our ideas, argue with authors, bounce issues back and forth, ask friends to read our early drafts, talk together after we've seen a movie, pass on books we've loved, attend meetings and argue things out, share stories and gossip that extend our understanding of ourselves and others. Talk lies at the heart of both our everyday lives and our intellectual development. This kind of exchange is rarely allowed in school or modeled there—not between kids or between adults. Most monthly faculty meetings are no better imitations of true discussion than the average so-called classroom discussion. One powerful motivation for becoming learned—that we might influence others—is purposely removed from students and their teachers. No one among the powerful policymakers wonders, as they imagine the perfect curriculum, what it means to teach a subject year after year following someone else's design. We organize schools as though the ideal was an institution impervious to human touch.

If we intend to dramatically improve the education of American kids, teachers must be challenged to invent schools they would like to teach and learn in, organized around the principles of learning that we know matter. That's the simple idea that teachers are beginning to put into practice in schools like the Urban Academy or International or the dozens of other new schools in New York City.

Just as the student body at CPESS is not exceptional but reflects the general population of New York City schools, our faculty are no more learned than the average teacher in the city, and certainly no more experienced. Many had almost no prior experience as teachers; some had taken courses in teaching. Many started as interns with us, spending their first year in a low-paid assistant teaching role; some came from other schools. But they all came with a willingness to learn from each other. Although often vulnerable, prickly, and defensive, they have all grown incredibly in the process of becoming better teachers. Today many speak about our work all over the country, something we consciously committed ourselves as a faculty to help each other learn to do. Others write about our work. They all see themselves first as the teachers of a particular group of youngsters, but they also see themselves as the governing body of a school and the carriers of an idea.

As my colleague Ann Bussis, a onetime researcher at Educational Testing Service, said, "Teaching is not so complex as to verge on the impossible or to defy conception at an abstract level, but it does defy concrete prescriptions for action. . . . There is neither prescription for action nor checklists for observation to assure intelligent and responsive teaching. All that can be offered are a guiding theory and abundant examples."

Dear students, parents and staff

We're back to business as usual. School starts again at 8 A.M.; the new term is under way. Hopefully, it'll be more than "business as usual." It's always our hope that there's at least one course, one topic within a course, one author, one teacher or one friend that will make a difference each year.

Sometimes it's even just a single conversation, or a single image. I read an article last week by Kenneth Freeston in *Education Week*. Freeston was a college sophomore when a senior said to him, "I have a theory about why . . ." "It was a night that changed my education," he writes. "Until then I studied only other people's theories. It was the first time I realized that being educated— learning—meant thinking for myself."

That's how we at CPESS define being well-educated: getting in the habit of developing theories that can be articulated clearly and then checked out in a thoughtful way. Of course, people who come up with good theories are people who are knowledgeable. You can't have a theory about baseball if you don't know the game. Good theorists are close observers who are always in the process of wondering why, putting things together and taking them apart! The things they put together and take apart differ: some of us theorize more about people, others more about cars. Some about history, others about numbers.

But one thing all good learners need theories about is their own way of learning. Schooling ends early in our life, but learning goes on and on and on. So being a theorist about oneself *as a learner* is critical.

An exercise: Make up three sentences beginning, "I have a theory that . . ." Most theories never get "proven," but act as "working hypotheses." So don't worry if you can't prove your theory. It's usually easier to disprove it! And a disproven theory is worth a lot—it can stop cluttering up your mind. So, after listing three theories, select one and write down what kind of evidence might disprove your theory.

I have a theory that this exercise is going to be very hard to do. How can that statement be disproven? Drop me a list of your theories!

CPESS NEWSLETTER

December 14

I just read the kids' journals in my advisory. I asked them to write down our own five "habits of mind"—which are listed on every classroom wall, discussed every week in our newsletter, used to organize curriculum, and are the basis for our "standards" for graduation. (How do you know what you know? What's your evidence? How and where does what you've learned "fit in"? Could things have been otherwise? Who cares, what difference does it make?) Only two kids out of ten remember any of them. I'm aghast. I start thinking we should have kids memorize them—although we ourselves never word them exactly the same way twice.

When we're trying to influence people's politics we recognize how difficult it is to dislodge a well-entrenched paradigm, a sustaining myth, an organizing principle. But when we "teach" we have to keep reminding ourselves that students are doing the same thing. They're screening out key points based on assumptions that we're not aware they hold; they're fitting new knowledge into old schemas where it isn't appropriate. Researchers have demonstrated this over and over. But our paradigm of teaching and learning is so well lodged that we don't hear the evidence! "Teaching is telling, learning is remembering." If we could just say it better, the kids would finally "get it." We focus on telling, not on listening.

Of course, the more engaged they are, the less passive their relationship to schooling, the better our chances. The more they make us listen. It's not enough to "want to do well." There's got to be a willingness to take risks. How rare is it for a student to say thoughtfully, "I just don't get it." And persist. Most kids are not lazy or unmotivated. But they don't know how, for example, to put in ten hours of homework. Most kids do homework like I did piano practice. One eye on the clock, practicing bad habits. Good "habits of mind" are not easy to catch on to.

JOURNAL

December 16

One of the teachers showed me as letter from Cheneta, who graduated last year. She's now at Cornell. Says Cheneta, "Those five CPESS habits of mind are proving very useful here." They "set us aside as special," said another student in a letter I got last week. People are "impressed," one kid quipped with a grin when he visited. (He's admitting he's bought in a little?)

Mike Rose, in *Lives on the Boundary*, walks the reader through his own initiation into the world of ideas. His apprenticeship. That's what a good school is: an apprenticeship into ideas. Learning to say "I've got a theory!" Somehow, somewhere, young people need to join, if only part-time, the club we belong to. That's more critical than the particulars of what they learn. But most of the time they are resisting membership—either out of fear of rejection or because to join such a club means to reject their own community or peer clubs. Or because they just don't "get it" yet, or "who wants it!"

It goes against the grain to see this as our job. It's why we are so hypercritical. It's not what we're "spozed" to be doing. We feel we have to justify the time spent listening to and observing kids or engaging them in endless conversation or asking them to "write it again" and again. Shouldn't we be covering more?! Won't they seem illiterate if we don't get to? Shouldn't we be pouring more in, instead of spending so much time stirring up what's already there? We drive each other mad spotting gaps—this kid doesn't use commas right, that one can't even remember the date of the Civil War! What kind of school *are* we?

January 25

Saturday. Our SAT [Scholastic Aptitude Test] scores came in. Half above 790, half below. Once again they are largely a measure of the social class of our students. Plus race. Despite the coaching. Over 90 percent of this year's potential graduates took them. Is it fair to encourage them all to take these tests? I suppose it's a measure of their hopefulness (or naivete) that they persist after low PSAT [Preliminary Scholastic Aptitude Test] scores. And we aren't good at discouraging kids. Last month the *New York Times* published ETS [Educational Testing Service] data showing how closely scores correlate with family income. Their graph grossly understates the case. The real social class disparities are much more devastating because so few students in the low-income categories take the test, and those who do are those rare high-achieving students who are considering expensive four-year colleges that care about SATs. Less than half of New York City's seniors take SATs, and only about half of the city's students ever reach their senior year! So we're comparing all our students to the top 25 percent.

The SAT overwhelmingly measures class. But is this because of bad schools or bad testing? Is it part and parcel of the test design? Or because the impact of the school is always limited?

When it gets down to individuals, the mismatch between SAT scores and real intellectual competence is shockingly clear. Leona's 890 is such an inadequate statement of her exceptional intellectual ability. The wound to children's confidence and self-respect is enormous. If I could raise their scores in any way I knew how, I would, just to ease their pain. Attacking the testmakers doesn't relieve the burden of self-doubt.

JOURNAL

9 It's Academic: Why Kids Don't Want to Be "Well-Educated"

The goal is not choice, school site autonomy, more resources, or more authentic forms of assessment. The goal is educating, and that means knowing what we're educating *for*. Purposes must be decided upon. As long as we avoid defining "why," our educational talk rings hollow. Even on the most practical level, until the kids know the destination getting there will be hard. And there's no way they can know if their parents and their teachers don't know. Too often we don't.

It's not enough to keep saying our goal is "academic excellence" as though that means something sufficiently neutral and obvious that none can disagree. It doesn't. At a time when we're proposing major change, confusion over terminology is more distracting and troublesome than it is in ordinary times. We need to replace the word "academic" with a new word, maybe more than one, for what we're after—with language that carries a different set of connotations.

A Martian on a visit to New York City might imagine that we are preparing a million children for a lifetime of academic scholarship. After all, she'd conclude, if you sent kids to a school that placed cooking or the violin at the central core of required courses, it would be to train students to become cooks or violinists. So it must be that we're grooming everyone to be academics. Yes? No? The Martian and the average student both deserve an answer. We need to reexamine the purpose of education.

Young people have always had only the foggiest notion of what schools are all about once the 3 R's stage is completed. Even the 3 R's mostly have stood for skill at schooling, only loosely connected, if at all, to anything you do elsewhere. What you did in first grade was mostly to get you ready for second, and in the second to prepare you for third. Even kindergarteners insist that you go to school for the purpose of school, not because adults use the skills and knowledge you learn there in the "real world." But in the past, when boredom or incompetence at schools-only skills got intolerable no one stopped youngsters from dropping out; in fact many encouraged it. Six or eight years of imposed drudgery, learning some only half useful rote skills from an adult only slightly better educated than their oldest charges was endurable if barely so (playing hooky has always been a widespread practice), but to put up with twelve years of serious high-stakes study young people have to want to be there, they need to be engaged learners. That's the rub!

To quote Joseph Priestley on the occasion of the dedication of New College in London in 1794,

> Whatever be the qualifications of your tutors, your improvement must chiefly depend on yourselves. They cannot think or labour for you, they can only put you in the best way of thinking and labouring for yourselves. If therefore you get knowledge you must acquire it by your own industry. You must form all conclusions and all maxims for yourselves, from premises and data collected and considered by yourself. And it is the great object of this institution to remove every bias the mind may be under, and to give the greatest scope for true freedom of thinking and equity.

He has summed up our problem and its solution. If the goal is becoming self-learners on behalf of "true freedom of thinking and equity," then the means must be one's own hard work.

Under such circumstances, what our students think about our

enterprise, whether it makes sense to them, is at the heart of the matter. If their schooling chiefly depends on *their* industry, then we must engage their industry. Until they see themselves as parties to their own education—as Mike Rose says so eloquently in *Lives on the Boundary*—they will not cross the divide. They need a bridge that connects their understanding of the meanings of the world to the ones being offered by "capital E Education." That's assuming Education is something worth crossing the boundary to get! How many students see it that way? How many of us could explain it to them?

Years ago I traveled to Spain with a friend. We went to the Prado (visiting museums was part of the expected rite of traveling). We got there late, and after an hour or so the guard reminded us the museum would soon be closing. I was sorry since my companion's greater interest in art was enlivening the experience of looking at art for me and I was enjoying it more than usual.

But I was unprepared for her reaction. I could tell that our required departure was creating genuine pain. She was experiencing something I didn't "get." The only way to relieve her discomfort was to assure her we'd go back first thing in the morning. "It means that much to you?" I asked. She was as surprised by my lack of feeling as I was by the power of hers. We stood, the two of us, on different sides of a divide that I knew no way to cross. I had never known a painting in the way she did. But for the first time in my life I recognized—and envied—what art could mean for others.

It was an experience that I relived from the other side a few years later when I remarked to a group of adults in a course I was teaching that I was late because I had hated to leave my car—I was right in the middle of listening to a Mozart quintet on the radio. There was a silence and finally one student asked, "Do you really listen to Mozart for pleasure?" She understood why classical music might improve one's mood or improve one culturally, but she couldn't imagine how such dry and remote music could arouse passion in me. That was unfathomable.

In part, many kids don't want to be "well-educated" because they can't even imagine what it is that could be "wantable." Which is not to say they don't want the credential, so they try. Ruth is compliant, has turned back to me her third draft, and now stares uncomprehendingly at the low grade and the many suggestions I've made on her paper. "But I did what you told me. I added two details. I changed the ending." Yet it's still all wrong and how am I to explain? There's something involved that she still just doesn't get. By now she's a little suspicious of us and our fancy standards. Are we pretending, as my adult students wondered about me and Mozart? Why are we so obstinately standing in the way of her getting a diploma? Her discouragement is compounded by the fact that she doesn't see the connection between the skills and knowledge needed to get the CPESS certificate and the skills and knowledge needed to hold the particular job that she hopes will follow. And surely she doesn't see the inherent pleasure of learning to write well, much less "academically." It's true that kids practice shooting baskets on their own for hours without asking what good it will do them. But of course we'd be surprised if kids who saw no relationship between their practice and their improvement or between shooting baskets and the game of basketball (much less kids who couldn't imagine being basketball players and had never seen a real game) devoted hours to practicing the sport.

So too with schooling. Too many kids don't see a connection between their efforts and school success, don't know what it is they need to practice, can't imagine themselves ever being "academic," and have never seen "academics" played. They're like I was at the Prado, but without my faith in the reality and desirability of my friend's passion.

But we're all guilty of having confused kids and ourselves by claiming what we're after is "academic," when we know that isn't quite true. We've defined being well-educated in terms of this word for so long and are so accustomed to it that it's a hard habit to break. And it's hard to imagine what to replace it with.

"Academic" is just a word, friends tell me. Why get so hung up on it? But "just a word" can cause a lot of damage. "Academic" has various specialized and very loaded meanings, also slippery ones. It's first of all ubiquitous, and it sends subliminal messages, often unintended, that we aren't aware of. Art and music, for example, are not "academic" unless we sever their connection from performance—from doing. Then we can have what's now called academic art. But why is "doing" nonacademic? And why is art worthier of school time when it's academic than when it's not? And why is science at least four times more important than even academic art? I once figured out that there are more jobs in New York City for people with advanced musical or artistic skills than for those with advanced calculus. But, see! I've fallen into the trap of assuming school is vocational. Okay, which do more citizens get pleasure from? Which leads them into improved habits of citizenship? I'd be hard put to claim calculus the winner over art or music on any such measure of real-life utility.

Everyone agrees history is an academic subject. Once it's so defined, we take it for granted it should be required. But why? Because if you don't study history you'll be doomed to repeat it? Do we truly believe that historians are better able to avoid repeating mistakes, or that nations with more historical knowledge have done better than those with less? (I can quickly think of several glaring examples of quite the reverse.) Perhaps the study of our common history, as E. D. Hirsch suggests, offers a unifying "common language" to all citizens, a sense of oneness? I know an alternate common language that would be a lot easier and cheaper to teach—the language of advertising and TV.

In fact, the claim that particular academic disciplines are sufficiently "good for you" to merit their present obligatory status is based on the barest of evidence. The study of algebra, for example, is justified by claims that (1) it's good exercise for the mind, (2) we all really need it to survive in modern society, (3) like it or not, it's a prerequisite for higher skilled jobs and thus a necessity to prevent being closed out of such opportunities if and when, and (4) it sets you apart from the uneducated. Most of us who studied algebra and were even good at it can't remember the last time we solved a problem using an algebraic equation. Teachers who claim to be well educated are quick to acknowledge that they don't know a thing about advanced math and don't intend to remedy this failure (although their students are required to). And if everyone did learn it, whatever "it" is, it wouldn't be useful for selection purposes. Hard-data freaks, measurement folks, arise! Find us some statistics that show a hard connection between the academic subjects taught in most high schools and successful living by anyone's standard, aside from the arbitrary connection we've created by making the one a prerequisite for the other. You need calculus to become an architect, and advanced math to go on to premed; but my brother, an architect, tells me he has never used calculus, and as for my doctor—*calculus*?

We spend years teaching paper-and-pencil arithmetic and make it a gatekeeper to more advanced math—rather than teaching our students to depend on calculators—because (we're told) suppose you don't have access to a calculator? We act as though the long division system we all learned was not itself an artificial crutch—what would we do without paper and pencil? The Chinese have survived for millennia using the abacus instead of our paper-and-pencil algorithms. Only mental arithmetic is truly independent of technology. Math educator Marilyn Burns is noted for reminding us that we don't keep a horse and carriage in our garage just in case our car breaks down. In fact we teach standard math because Americans think "it's academic" (that is, conventional) to know your times tables. We teach certain more prestigeful forms of math at CPESS for similar reasons, to make freshman college math teachers happy, to pass tests, to beat the gatekeepers, and, I'm embarrassed to admit, to "look good." The Academy rules. Other perhaps more useful forms of mathematical literacy—statistics and probability, for example—get short-changed. You just can't do everything! It's bad enough to have to do this to the students who go on to college, but it's doubly unfair to those who choose not to.

I'm pushing this point, playing with all these examples even in such a sacrosanct area as math, because I suspect that until we accept the challenge to find better criteria for defining what's worth knowing we're going to keep going around in circles. Don't I want them to study subject matter? Yes! Am I arguing that algebra is too hard for ordinary kids? No! I'm not decrying a focus on facts, information, subject matter, or even memorization, much less rigor. As far as I know statistics is as rigorous as algebra or calculus, even if the latter is more "academic."

And I believe in facts. If you look bewildered by the expression "three strikes you're out," have never heard of Lou Gehrig (or think that's only the same of a rare disease), think there have always been twenty-eight major league baseball teams, then your theories about the game probably won't be worth hearing out. "Wonderful ideas," Eleanor Duckworth reminds us, "do not spring out of nothing." Close observation, attention to detail, having information ready to use and the know-how to use it are the heart of any well-performed trade, academic or nonacademic. Including the trade of citizen! That's what schools must "teach."

Furthermore, I want *all* kids to know that the heritage of academia—including calculus—belongs to them as much as to anyone else. And they won't learn this by shying away from such fields, especially in a culture that has traditionally put off-limits signs on academic subjects for the least advantaged of our fellow citizens—"Sorry, but this is not meant for you." That's why it's necessary to get our language straight. Until we do we reinforce the belief that "academics" are intended at one and the same time to be irrelevant to the concerns of most people and far too important and rigorous for them. We demand that everyone study traditional academics if they want to succeed but expect few to really "get it" because it's too dry and abstract. We spend endless hours training students to write "academic prose," and those who get to be good at it then spend endless hours in "real life" unlearning what most consider an ineffective writing style. It's rarely praise to have one's writing called academic. We've defined the word so that its antonyms are "useful" and "popular." That's called a double-bind!

But academia is not meant, I hear a voice whispering in me, to be relevant, useful, practical. Trying to make it so will corrupt it. Beyond a certain point, the whisper persists, it's not meant for all ordinary people, it doesn't have to be popular. It's a very special vocation which few are called to serve; not everything worth doing need meet such a standard of utility and universality as you're demanding. I hear the whisper and I concur—up to a point.

If we accept an academic tradition that doesn't justify itself by its usefulness, that's fine. But we can't then simultaneously insist that all young people spend twelve years devoted almost exclusively to its demands. There are sounder ways to maintain the integrity and health of academic learning than making it the gatekeeper for all other "worthy" adult activities. Once we recognize and acknowledge that academia is but one form of intellectual life, we can begin to imagine the other possibilities. Other possibilities don't mean that all traditional disciplines are now unimportant to us; quite the opposite, they force us to ask how such disciplines are relevant to our inquiries. They make the discipline, however, second to the intellectual inquiry. What determines what we study, the driving criteria, should be the demands of a democratic citizenry, not the requirements of academia.

Based on such criteria I'd argue, for example, that all students need to understand the way scientists arrive at truth. They need opportunities to experience the scientific method in operation precisely because they can't be expected to reinvent modern science in their own spare time. No matter how gifted they may be, much must be taken on authority. Students need reasons to respect the conclusions reached by those who work at science full time, reasons other than the belief that it's another form of "received truth." The trick is to teach them this confidence in the scientific establishment in ways that support the use of scientific thought in their own lives, as well as the capacity to hazard an opinion on matters of science that may pertain to political and moral priorities, and a healthy and knowing skepticism toward the misuse of scientific authority. Have I a package ready that will accomplish *all* of these sophisticated goals? No. But the teaching methods most widely used now accomplish none of them. They fill us instead with a vast undigested array of facts and theories that college-level science departments have proclaimed to be essential (which we rarely remember or remember wrongly) and a lasting susceptibility to superstition and false or un-substantiated scientific claims.

We have unwittingly allowed "academic" to become a synonym for the right stuff when we're talking about schooling. (And only when we're talking schooling.) Academic equals tough, valued. To be nonacademic is to admit to low standards or to mushy ones. A course that claims to be practical is by definition of lower value, a "soft" course. The more intriguing and inherently interesting the course title, the less likely it is to be considered "serious." New York City is about to launch a requirement that all students take three years of academic math and academic science, more than were re-quired for even the most elite students in either field when I was a youngster. Ironically, at a time when mathematicians are urging an infusion of practical applications into course work, school people are trying to "raise standards" by further estranging theory from practice. The latest rage for schools who fear they won't be taken seriously is to call themselves "academies." And on and on. Such ma-nipulations through language are sloppy and damaging. They take our minds away from what's really happening in our schools and classes while we play with labels and titles.

Is there other language that will do better by us? The advantage of the word "intellectual," for example, is that it is not particular to the campus, to universities, or even to people who were trained there; it hasn't yet been filled with school-based jargon. "Using one's mind well," Ted Sizer reminds us, is a practical essential like good health and is exhibited as much in the conduct of a good craftsman's life as in a mathematician's. Shifting our language only helps, of course, if it stimulates some fresh thought. It could help if it made us reconsider why we believe adding to one's knowledge and mas-tering certain classroom skills are legitimate school objectives but producing a play, tutoring younger children, editing the school newspaper, or writing for the poetry magazine are extracurricular. Do such activities lose their inherent need for rigor, skill, or knowl-edge because they are authentic? If so, how will we reconcile the re-cent interest in "authentic assessment" with our increased demands for "academic rigor"? We're ruled by an archaic set of categories that have a history and purpose that confounds our students, and us. We slip from one to another mindlessly. When one is caught between two worlds, it's generally necessary to reframe the issues.

We need to invent a new learned tradition with goals that we honor and that all who strive for can achieve, to replace an old tradition which few took seriously and only some could by definition succeed in.

We might even want all our young people to be intellectuals—*all* of them. That's where my vote would go. Beauticians and plumbers as well as lawyers and doctors. CPESS's strategy rests on its definition of purpose: putting all our young people in a position to explore and act upon the fundamental intellectual and social issues of their times.

If we agree that what we want are citizens with a lively curiosity—who ask, How come? and, Why? and, Is it truly so?—we'll have the start of a new definition of "well-educated." How about being closely *observant*, prepared to keep one's eyes and ears open for patterns, for details, for the unusual? Schooling should encourage *playfulness*—the capacity to imagine, to wonder, to put things together in new and interesting ways—as well as the possession of a *skeptical and open mind*. To be in the habit of *imagining how others think*, feel, and see the world—in the habit of stepping into the shoes of others—should surely be one of our new basics. (How else, after all, can we follow the Golden Rule?) And of course we need to be *respectful of evidence*, to distinguish good data from bad, to hesitate before sounding off without any facts. I'd add *knowing how to communicate* carefully, persuasively, and powerfully in a variety of media—including the skilled use of written and spoken language. My definition would also put a high premium on *caring* enough about the world and one's fellow citizens to take a stand and defend it.

My definition will also honor *the work ethic*. It was one of the main (if not only) values that the old diploma once served—marking as it did the capacity to stick it out. It's easy to scoff at mere "seat-time," but we fool ourselves when we pretend that employers aren't still at least as concerned over work habits as they are over so-called cognitive skills and academic knowledge. It's not only old-fashioned factories that care about punctuality; reliability is not passé. And such habits of work are also important in a friend, a neighbor, a mate, a colleague. No community can survive if its members can't count on each other.

This short laundry list of qualities is so far intentionally agnostic about particular disciplines of academia. It neither endorses them or dismisses them. But it takes as its starting point the fact that academia has no monopoly on the habits of mind that underlie good practice in all vocations in a democratic society, including the first and foremost of vocations, that of citizen. If we get it right, a new focus will elevate respect for academia and improve the economy to boot but won't be determined by either.

The alternatives that work may not abandon traditional academic schooling, but they rarely use it as their starting point. The work of Foxfire is such an example—an approach to teaching through involving students in authentic local history that grew out of the work of one teacher in one rural Appalachian community and became a national phenomenon. But programs based on Foxfire remain a sideshow in too many cases, a special treat, not a challenge to the whole idea of schooling. The work of the Coalition of Essential Schools is another example. While it defends the principle of "less is more," Coalition schools—over seven hundred nationwide—are struggling over how to decide which "less" is worth more.

If our definition of an educated person is made broader than the one we're now accustomed to, if we see traditional academics as but one example of important intellectual activity, not a synonym for such activity, then possibilities open up for us. If habits are the goal, then things other than the academic disciplines themselves can serve as subject matter. For example, in our elementary school some students study bridges for several months as an exploration of physical structures, geometric patterns, the relationship between form and function, the history of communities, and the relationship between technology and social history. They create, invent, examine, observe, read, interview, design and measure. In the high school, students spend a year looking at the question of "who's an American" in all its different meanings, which requires a study of history, culture, psychology, geography and politics, literature and the visual arts. Students spend months, sometimes years, with variants of the question of whether what's good for the planet earth and what's good for the human species are synonymous. Is this science? Social studies? Philosophy? Morality?

Human beings, for all our terrible flaws, are by nature theorists, thinkers. Our theory-making capacity is connected to the fact that we are a species that gets pleasure out of sense-making. Yes, pleasure—watch an infant at work turning the world into a predictable place. We're also capable, although this takes cultivation, of sustaining uncertainty, of postponing immediate gratification—the quick answer. That odd combination of hubris and humility essential to intellectual work is tenuous, a fragile balancing act, but it's within the grasp of all of us. These traits are the hard-won habits of mind, work, and heart that are both natural and in some ways unnatural, requiring cultivation—in other words, schooling.

The practical problems that a reframed discussion of what's worth studying raises will not be easy to solve. At CPESS we think we're still only tiptoeing around the issue. We're all constrained by wondering how it translates onto a college application form, whether kids will feel cheated when their college teacher is outraged at what they didn't "cover," and by our own conservatism about changing traditions that might serve uses we haven't yet understood. But we are also sure that while shifting pedagogical styles is important it won't solve the problem unless we also look at *what* we teach. While teaching the traditional academic material well always helps and is only minimally harmful in a practical sense for students who take to it easily, the price for others—even with good teaching—is enormous. There's no way to spend the time needed on strong intellectual habits if one is whizzing through academic terrain at the speed required to cover it, and no way to engage all young people when the choice of subject matter isn't rooted in real inquiry on the part of teachers and students alike. As Joseph Priestley said in 1794, the effort required to learn can only take place when we enlist the industry of our students. They've got to see that it matters. Because it does.

December 12

I shoo Felicida out of the bathroom where she and a friend are fixing their hair—five minutes after class has started. I next see her banging on a door that says PLEASE USE OTHER DOOR. THIS IS NOT AN ENTRANCE. I point to the sign and to the proper entrance. I next see her banging on *that* door. I go over and quietly open the door (it's not locked). She enters loudly. The teacher gives us an angry "Why are you interrupting this class?" look. I realize Felicida doesn't belong in this room but has come in to collect her coat and bookbag! I tell her in a whisper to come across to the office to talk to me. She gets nasty, belligerent, and tries out all her "attitudes" on me. Why doesn't she seem scared? I go from calm old lady to furious defied authority. I leave her, to recapture my composure. I bring back all her records and we peruse them together. Her physical posture shifts. She allows a smile. She meets my eye. She accepts my role as giver of lessons. The chip on her shoulder shifts. It has taken more than an hour of my day. But we're both happy. I think it's a breakthrough. Still, we'll see.

JOURNAL

January 9

Jose has, as usual, come to school hours late. I threaten. I call home. I remind him that it's our job to "teach" but his job (and his family's) to get to school. (Actually it's a poor way to pose it, since it sounds as though I mean that once he gets here we do all the work! Once again the language of schooling is based on a notion of teaching and learning that's all wrong!)

But he still comes in late. He's daring me to kick him out. What would be the point of it? Even if I could! (I can't.)

The "free schoolers" insist that as long as it's mandatory it won't work. There's a sense in which they are right. There's nothing unworkable or undemocratic about having mandated obligations to others. But if one doesn't "buy into them" they will not be done well.

So Jose, his adviser and I agree on a new plan that includes new penalties. Will we be conscientious enough to follow through or will he wear us out? We need to attend to the other side too. Is his failure to engage related to not knowing *how* to succeed in our school or because he has other more critical priorities in his life? Is our involvement with his family a mistake? As long as he sees family and school as together, does this mean he can't use school as an oasis from his family whom he is trying to distance himself from?

Tomorrow I meet with Yolanda about her pattern of lateness and absenteeism. In her case it's tied into her being a good daughter and sister. To her, school is a distraction from her central task: helping out those who love her and care for her. She smiles politely; there's steely disdain underneath it. At heart she's never with us. Doing well at school would require her to see us as allies. At present we seem at best a benign enemy (or nuisance), always telling her to make school her priority!

What differentiates these two from the ones who buy in fast?

JOURNAL

November 25

Rose, who works in the elementary school, says she saw Antonio buying or selling drugs last weekend. She isn't willing to be quoted on it. I understand although I suspect I could push her into it. Paul and I talk it over and decide to ask the adviser to call the family in. We'll tell them—with Antonio present—"We think it's true, but can't do anything about it whether it is or isn't, so felt we just needed to pass the rumor on to you." They may get mad and defensive and accuse us (since the kid is sure to deny it). Or they could be grateful and acknowledge that they've been worrying. Or something in between.

JOURNAL

November 26

We met with Antonio's family. He denied using or selling drugs, of course. But his mother trusted our story. These are the moments when the years of patient alliance between school and family pay off. We can help.

JOURNAL

February 13

Scientists, bless them, have "discovered" (*New York Times*, December 24) that there's a quality called "hopefulness" that is a better predictor of success, even in college, than grade-point average, class rank or SAT score! Maybe it's "hopefulness" that we keep alive at CPE. Maybe our success is not related to our highly praised curriculum or pedagogy but to creating an intensely personal and stable place that's always there for kids. The kids complain at times that we give (other) kids too many chances. They complain about how the teachers are always getting "into our business." They tell visitors we're "like a family." At times I deny this—because we are after all here for a purpose. We're not endlessly bound to love and forgive. But on the other hand: maybe it's in that gray area between being a family and a school that we engender hopefulness.

We need this midwinter break.

JOURNAL

10 On Failure, Persistence, and Public Education

I've been involved in starting three schools and intimately connected to the opening of a dozen more. Almost every one came close to extinction at least once in its first few years. Their troubles came from different sources: "too much" parental involvement or not enough, an overly controlling director or confusion over who's running the ship, and (of course) personality clashes with or without political overtones. And if these are not inevitable, one can count on unexpected blows. On June 1 of CPESS's first year, while waiting for the birth of my first grandchild, I got word by phone that a student had been run over on a school trip. I felt simultaneous fear for the boy's life and fear for the school's future. Fortunately, he survived with minimal damage (and was part of our first graduating class). If parenting is sometimes nerve-racking, in a community of hundreds one is always on the edge of disaster, a phone call away from tragedy.

Teaching, like parenting, sometimes feels more like a succession of near-misses, almosts, and downright failures. How honest are we as parents about our failings and doubts? To whom do we divulge our deepest worries? Threatened by exposure in the local newspaper, by regular postings of comparative parental success, would our willingness to open our doors and reflect on the truth increase or decrease? In the midst of our professional work at CPE, despite much praise, we see all the warts. And we open our doors nervously.

Kids change very slowly, and not always in quite the ways we were anticipating. On any particular day the possibilities of things going very awry are considerable. We find ourselves making the same dumb mistakes over and over. We try to remember not to lose our cool on Friday afternoon or it will bother us all weekend. And we hope no visitor hears us at our worst moments.

Two years ago I ambitiously decided to teach a senior course on New York history and politics, about which I thought I knew at least a bit. (And what I didn't know I thought my coteacher David Gartner, a young urban intern, knew as well as anyone.) Of the dozen students we started with, only half ended up getting course credit or using the work for their portfolios. There wasn't a teaching mistake we didn't make. We overplanned, as though by dint of spelling it all out we'd insure against the realities of twelve ornery adolescents. We underestimated the difficulty of our reading list. We were sure the kids would find things interesting on the basis of our enthusiasm alone. We expected they'd enjoy working together over weekends and holidays to explore neighborhoods that in fact they found intimidating. Fortunately, at the age of sixty I've learned to turn embarrassment into opportunity and we tried to use the experience to think aloud about our work. But it reminded me of how often I cried in my early years of teaching—and of being a director before I got a codirector. Tears of fear, frustration, anger, and sorrow.

There's never a time when one can say, Well, I've done all that can be done. There is always something else. A child you haven't done quite right for; a family that is in unnecessary distress because of school issues; a teacher you haven't been a help to; a book, a game, an idea that might turn the tide. It's a matter of endless lists, and none of the items are ever the kind you can cross off and put behind you. That conversation that you thought forever changed this child's distrust was after all just one step along the road toward a more trusting relationship. And then, in the midst of it all, comes an imperious call from someone "downtown" demanding compliance, asking, Who do you think you are? or, Where were you? or, How come?—and you feel outrage. Even when we get a better arrangement of power between school folks and school bureaucracies, we'll still have such irritations. (Private school headmasters have to deal with both state authorities and their boards of trustees.) What we can do is improve the odds that these phenomena don't drive out the best educators and undermine the natural drive to do one's best that lies at the heart of good parenting and good schooling. When we no longer believe such a natural drive exists, we've lost most of the battle. That's the "secret ingredient" that must be given an opportunity—plus a public nudge now and then—to take center stage in schooling.

It's thirty years since I began and twenty-one since Central Park East opened its doors. I feel almost as far from discovering how to make a difference as I did then. That sounds foolish, given our successes. But given what I wanted to do, it's a simple fact. The puzzle isn't, it turns out, one where you can finally put the last piece in and say "Done." It just gets more and more complicated. My first class had thirty-five kids and I had no helpers. My next class had twelve and I had a superb assistant. I was, in raw terms, "more successful" with the second class. But I was equally puzzled and equally "dissatisfied" by both. But my puzzlements and my dissatisfaction were of a different order.

There are, in the end, only two main ways human beings learn: by observing others (directly or vicariously) and by trying things out for themselves. Novices learn from experts and from experience. That's all there is to it. Everything else is in the details. Until we create schools in which the ratio of novices to experts is lower and the opportunities for novices to try out what they see and hear the experts doing are more plentiful, we'll be wasting much of our time. Until we, in whatever other roles we play in life, demonstrate our own dedication to the values we ask schools to demonstrate, the intellectual seriousness and thoughtfulness we want for our young will not be a commonplace school phenomenon. The experts needed include other students, books and movies, teachers and other adults—and not just in school. We also know that we don't learn from all experts (and Herb Kohl has written a great essay on this provocative topic, entitled "I Won't Learn from You"). Some we tune out and we don't always know why, but the way schools are positioned in the larger culture and society has something to do with how youngsters see and hear "school people" and their brand of smarts. How to create the right conditions and provide the appropriate practice and feedback will require endless finagling and thus endless opportunities to make both small and big mistakes.

As a parent I used to say that as long as two out of three kids were doing okay on any one day that was great, and one out of three was okay. It was the days on which all three seemed in a bad way that I would lose heart. And of course most of the time I was ignorant about how things were going and just sailed along smoothly. The advantage of a school, even a small one, is that it's easier to persevere because there's bound to be something right most days; on the other hand, there's less chance that no one will let you know when things are amiss.

Keeping a sense of humor is another requirement of both parenting and schoolteaching. Some people say it's also a characteristic of a healthy democratic society—that it can laugh at itself. Mostly, of course, one needs a sense of humor about all the grand schemes that grand people devise. For example, the latest vast schemes to see to it that all kids become what we wish we had been made to be! Or that they know what our learned college professors don't want to bother to teach and therefore want someone else to take care of first. It's interesting to note that when an international study points out that more than two thirds of all college teachers everywhere find their students "unprepared," few realize that this is a joke on the insularity of academia—Why aren't they more like me?—not proof of the orneriness of students or the lack of rigor in their schools.

As I read the latest batch of state and national "curriculum frameworks" and diploma requirements—written in that odd jargonese of "all students will . . ."—only a sense of humor keeps me sane. Imagine otherwise intelligent people getting together and publishing the following proclamations (taken from a proposed statewide curriculum and assessment mandate) that "all students will" by the end of tenth grade "learn to understand and cope with death and dying" and "with the myriad of problems associated with aging," "know how to establish, maintain, and end relationships," and "demonstrate an understanding of disease and disorders and take action to control, prevent, or limit and treat their development." The latter sounds like what an M.D. is expected (maybe) to "know and do." While curing the world's diseases our ninth-grader is also taking one semester of art, which will prepare him or her to "demonstrate ability in composing, arranging, and improving music," "play an ensemble instrument," know the major visual artists of his/her culture and others, and produce a one-act play. (By the time they graduate they will be able to choreograph a dance, improvise in various ethnic styles, and write and put on a "meaningful" three-act play.) Meanwhile, based on their ninth-grade global studies course, they will demonstrate "the connection between the pre–nation state, the development of nationalism and current geopolitical and economic issues" in Latin America, East, Central, and Southern Asia, the Mideast and Africa, along with literally a dozen other weighty theses. By the time they graduate high school they'll have mastered the "basics" that drive all of the academy, plus life itself, and have already earned mini-Ph.D.'s in a dozen fields of study.

My antidote is the new Meier Mandate: "No school shall have graduation requirements that cannot be met by every professional working in the school, and therefore these requirements shall be phased in only as fast as the school can bring its staff up to the standards it requires of its students." We're planning to test this one out at CPESS. School boards and legislatures might try it out on themselves, too.

But these too shall pass.

It would help, of course, if all our children had sound reasons to expect a decent and dignified job in the future, as well as neighborhoods and opportunities that offered them and their families a decent present. What would seem intolerable to any reader of this book should not have to be tolerated by any youngster in our great city or in the nation. In the end that's what still bothers me—it isn't fair. The unfairness cuts even deeper thirty years later, hurts more.

But there's also always hope—the fifty new small schools of

choice in New York City alone, all roughly consistent with the ideas laid out here, and another fifty that are on the drawing board for the future, and many others throughout the country. While policymakers and ideologues are busily inventing a new top-down fad every year or two—a uniform national curriculum, school prayer, or a system of private vouchers—there's a slow awakening among school people, things are taking root out there that may not be easy to stop. People *are* "having wonderful ideas" in the sense that Eleanor Duckworth celebrated in her book by that name. It may be possible to have small idiosyncratic schools, lots of autonomy, public accountability, a fair amount of equity, *and* schools that work! But it will require us to abandon the stance of "outsiders" in relation to schooling. We can't afford to attack others for getting involved just because we don't like their ideas. We need to cultivate the adult habit of getting involved.

It won't come as a surprise that I think the conditions that foster good teaching are the conditions I've described already: small schools, schools of choice, school autonomy over the critical dimensions of teaching and learning, lots of time for building relationships and reflecting on what's happening, along with a culture of mutual respect for others and a set of habits of mind that fosters inquiry as well as responsibility.

What makes me hopeful, no matter what bad news tomorrow brings, is our infinite capacity for inventing the future, imagining things otherwise. It's what allows me to remain optimistic even though there's presently more racism and meanness in my home town, and the nation, than I ever recall witnessing before—and teenagers in our city bear the brunt of both. There are opportunities out there; things are stirring. *It's up to parents and teachers to find their way into the current reform debate.* Change won't happen the way I've been describing if it depends on policymakers, big-name task forces, well-intentioned governors or systems thinkers. Change will take people who remember what otherwise gets lost: that it's not just about building a powerful America, beating out Japan, or even world-class job skills; it's about creating a more powerful citizenry and a more caring one. Even then we'll have lots to argue about. But it's about our kids and our shared future with them. Worth arguing about.

Luckily, in the meantime the work is interesting and tomorrow I just might figure out where this little piece over there goes . . . though I know that the puzzle is always changing shape. That's what's so marvelous about living things, they're never entirely predictable. They can always confound the odds.

Suggested Readings

The list below is suggestive. In some cases it includes one particular book or essay by an author, though there are many I'd equally recommend. In other cases I left off books or articles by authors I love because they overlap with the issues and ideas of others already included, and I wanted to keep this short. So use one source to lead you to others. And, of course, these are by the authors I mostly agree with. Reading the "others" is important too, but that's another list altogether!

Bracey, Gerald W. "The Bracey Report on the Condition of Public Education," *Phi Delta Kappan*, October 1991–94. (They've dealt successively with myths of a golden past, international comparisons, etc. See parallel work by David C. Berliner, *Phi Delta Kappan*, Fall 1993, or Larry Cuban, *Education Week*, June 15, 1994.)

Carini, Patricia F. "Images and Immeasurables." Occasional paper, Prospect Center, North Bennington, Vt., 1993. (A powerful, original, and highly influential thinker whose work begins with the close study of children at their place of work.)

Cohen, Dorothy. *The Learning Child*. New York: Schocken, 1972. (A classic on young children as learners.)

Darling-Hammond, Linda. "Reframing the School Reform Agenda," *Phi Delta Kappan*, June 1993, pp. 753–61 (One of dozens of great articles by the co-director of NCREST and the foremost expert in the field of teacher education and school policy reform.)

Delpit, Lisa. *Other People's Children: Cultural Conflict in the Classroom*. New York: New Press, 1994. (A continuation of important and provocative work over the past ten years.)

Dewey, John. *Democracy and Education*. New York: Free Press, 1965. (Or try *Education and Experience*—more lay-reader friendly perhaps.)

Duckworth, Eleanor. *The Having of Wonderful Ideas and Other Essays*. New York: Teachers College Press, 1987. (Gets to the heart of humans as learners and is delightful reading to boot.)

Fine, Michelle. *Chartering Urban School Reform: Reflecting on Public High Schools in the Midst of Change*. New York: Teachers College Press,

1984. (One of a number of provocative books and essays by one of a small crew of marvelous scholar-reformers.)

Freedman, Samuel. *Small Victories: The Real World of a Teacher.* New York: HarperCollins, 1992. (About one teacher in one big high school—teaching at its best under difficult circumstances.)

Glickman, Carl E. *Renewing America's Schools.* San Francisco: Jossey-Bass, 1993. (An unusually thoughtful "how-to" for democratic schooling, based on extensive first-hand experience.)

Gould, Stephen Jay. *The Mismeasure of Man.* New York: Norton, 1981. (Every generation the winners try to prove it's all in their genes. Gould's book is the best and most readable response and will probably do for several generations to come.)

Holt, John. *How Children Fail.* New York: Dell, 1968. (A 1960's classic that changed my life.)

Howe, Harold. *Thinking about Kids: An Agenda.* New York: Free Press, 1993. (Wisdom galore from America's eminent educator and activist.)

Kohl, Herbert R. *Thirty-Six Children.* New York: NAL-Dutton, 1988. (Reprint of the 1967 classic by an author who keeps writing classics, including his latest, *I Won't Learn from You*, New Press, 1994.)

Kozol, Jonathan. *Savage Inequalities.* New York: HarperCollins, 1992. (Clear and sharp and indignant details on who gets what in America's schools.)

Letter to a Teacher by Schoolboys of Barbiana, translated from Italian by Nora Rossi and Tom Cole. Postscript by Robert Coles and John Holt. New York: Random House, 1970. (An oldie; a reminder that we're not talking about a strictly American issue.)

Lieberman, Ann, ed. *The Work of Restructuring Schools: Building from the Ground Up.* New York: Teachers College Press (in press). (An important collection by NCREST's co-director; one of many she has edited.)

Little, Judith Warren. *Ties That Bind.* New York: Teachers College Press (in press). (All of her essays and collections, which focus on teachers as colleagues, are important and satisfying reading.)

Meier, Deborah. "Why Reading Tests Don't Test Reading," *Dissent*, Fall 1981, pp. 457–66. (How we define and measure success is not a neutral technical exercise. Until we understand the nature of norm-referenced testing—reading tests or IQ tests—we'll not get far. I wrote this a long time ago, but it still says what I mean.)

Mitchell, Lucy Sprague. *The Young Geographers*. New York: Bank Street College of Education, 1991 reprint. (An old classic; this is what good teaching is like—in marvelous readable detail.)

Paley, Vivian. *Wally's Stories: Conversations in the Kindergarten*. Cambridge, Mass.: Harvard University Press, 1981. (By a kindergarten teacher whose books are all important windows into children's ideas.)

Perrone, Vito. *A Letter to Teachers: Reflections on Schooling and the Art of Teaching*. San Francisco: Jossey-Bass, 1991. (Perrone has been the steadiest giant in the reform field—a doer, historian, and friend to teachers and parents everywhere. He's now at Harvard.)

Rose, Mike. *Lives on the Boundary*. New York: Viking Penguin, 1990. (A breakthrough account of what it takes to cross over from the "other side of the tracks" in terms of academic literacy. See also *Possible Lives* [in press], about good teaching in America.)

Sarason, Seymour. *The Culture of School and the Problem of Change*. Boston: Allyn and Bacon, 1982. (Anything Sarason writes is a "must read," but this was his seminal work on the topic.)

Seletsky, Alice. "Where the Action Is," *The Nation*, May 25, 1985. (A great teacher's account of why we do it.)

Shulman, Lee. "Aristotle Had It Right: On Knowledge and Pedagogy." Occasional paper no. 4, The Holmes Group, Michigan State University, May 1990. (Shulman, now at Stanford, is an eminent learning theorist—see also "Knowledge and Teaching," *Harvard Educational Review*, vol. 57, 1987. He is also one of a small coterie of experts who have been trying to find a way to use assessment—the field of psychometrics—to expand our knowledge, not just sort kids. See the work of Ted Chittenden of ETS, Pamela Moss of the University of Michigan, Walt Haney, George Madaus, and others.)

Sizer, Ted. *Horace's Compromise: The Dilemma of the American High School*. Boston: Houghton Mifflin, 1992. (See also *Shopping Mall High*, by Arthur Powell, et al., and *The Last Little Citadel*, by Robert Hampel, on the story of American high schools since 1940. This Houghton Mifflin threesome provides the background for the creation of the Coalition of Essential Schools.)

Smith, Frank. *Reading without Nonsense*. New York: Teacher's College Press, 1985. (All his books on literacy are stunning. This is probably the most readable and critical to understanding literacy and learning.)

Articles, Books, and Videos about the Central Park East Schools

Ancess, Jacqueline, et al. "The Development of Authentic Assessment at Central Park East Secondary School," *Creating Learner-Centered Accountability*. New York: The National Center for Restructuring Education, Schools, and Teaching, 1993.**

Bensman, David. *Lives of the Graduates of Central Park East Elementary School. Where Have They Gone? What Did They Really Learn?* New York: The Center for Collaborative Education and the National Center for Restructuring Education, Schools, and Teaching, 1994.*

———. *Quality Education in the Inner City: The Story of the Central Park East Schools*. New York: The Center for Collaborative Education, 1987.*

Darling-Hammond, Linda, et al. *Graduation by Portfolio at Central Park East Secondary School*. New York: The National Center for Restructuring Education, Schools, and Teaching (in press).**

Fliegel, Sy, and James MacGuire. *Miracle in East Harlem: The Fight for Choice in Public Education*. New York: Random House, 1993.

Graduation by Portfolio—Performance-Based Assessment at Central Park East Secondary School. 50 minutes.*

Snyder, Jon, et al. *Makers of Meaning in a Learner-Centered School: A Case Study of Central Park East I Elementary School*. New York: The National Center for Restructuring Education, Schools, and Teaching, 1992.**

Wiseman, Fred. *High School II*. 220 minutes.***

Wood, George, Ph.D. *Schools That Work—America's Most Innovative Public Education Programs*. New York: Penguin, 1992.

For further information, please contact:

*The Center for Collaborative
Education
1573 Madison Avenue,
Room 201
New York, NY 10029
(212) 348-7821

**The National Center for
Restructuring Education,
Schools, and Teaching
Box 110, Teachers College
Columbia University
New York, NY 10027
(212) 678-3432

***Zipporah Films
1 Richdale Avenue, Unit 4
Cambridge, MA 02140
(617) 576-3603